Storrs Lectures on Jurisprudence
Yale Law School, 1974

The Ages of
American Law

Grant Gilmore

New Haven and London   Yale University Press

Published with assistance from the foundation
established in memory of Oliver Baty Cunningham
of the Class of 1917, Yale College.

Designed by John O. C. McCrillis
and set in Times Roman type.
Printed in the United States of America by
BookCrafters, Inc., Chelsea, Michigan.

Library of Congress Cataloging in Publication Data

Gilmore, Grant.
    The ages of American law.
    (Storrs lectures on jurisprudence; 1974)
    Includes index.
    1. Law—United States—History and
criticism—Addresses, essays, lectures.   I. Title.
II. Series.
KF352.A2G5   340'.0973   76–49988
ISBN 0–300–01951–3 cloth
        0–300–02352–9 paper

20 19 18 17 16

Contents

Preface

In 1972 the dean and faculty of the Yale Law School invited me to deliver a series of lectures on the Storrs Foundation. The lectures were scheduled for October 1974 on the occasion of a convocation which marked the hundred and fiftieth anniversary of the Law School's founding. The timing suggested to me as an appropriate subject a review of American law during the century and a half of at times uneasy coexistence of the Yale Law School and the American legal system.

This book is an expanded version of the 1974 Storrs Lectures.[1] It is not—any more than the original lectures were—a contribution to the scholarly literature. I have put forward a number of hypotheses about what seems to have happened in American law since 1800 or thereabouts along with some speculations about why what seems to have happened should have happened. My hypotheses and speculations make a certain amount of sense to me. I shall be pleased if they make any sense to others. I have, however, made no attempt to "prove" the soundness of my views by the piling up of conventional documentation. The notes will serve to guide the curious reader to other discussions of some of the issues here passed in review.

My own area of expertise lies in what is usually referred to as commercial law (which, as lawyers use the term, includes the general law of contracts). The illustrations and analogies which come most readily to my

mind are drawn from the material I am familiar with.
If I had been an expert in criminal law or constitutional
law, the illustrations and analogies would have been
drawn from those fields. The book would, in that case,
have had a different flavor; I doubt that the argument
would have been substantially different from the one
that is here presented.

GRANT GILMORE

Yale Law School

Acknowledgments

I am most grateful to former Dean Abraham Goldstein and the faculty of the Yale Law School for the invitation to give the lectures on which this book is based. Dean Goldstein sat patiently through all three of the lectures — a courtesy which, I thought, was well above and beyond the scope of his duty.

I am indebted to many of my students at the Yale Law School for thoughtful suggestions and helpful criticisms in seminar papers and discussions over the past few years. In particular I should like to thank David Roe, who read over the original text of the lectures and made a great many useful comments; Philip Bobbitt, who contributed both an introduction to and editorial supervision of the lecture which was published in the *Yale Law Journal* as "The Age of Anxiety" (84 *Yale L.J.* 1022 (1975)); James D. Miller, who first drew my attention to the parallelism between the ideas of Holmes and Peirce in a paper which was published as "Holmes, Peirce, and Legal Pragmatism" (84 *Yale L.J.* 1123 (1975)); Charles Yablon, for a paper, which so far as I know has not been published, on the philosophical bases of Holmes's book, *The Common Law*.

Andrew Kossover, of the Vermont Law School, provided valuable assistance in research and showed great ingenuity and resourcefulness in running down out-of-the-way sources and references.

I also owe a debt of appreciation to Eileen Quinn and the secretarial staff of the Yale Law School, to Bea Ericson and the secretarial staff of the Vermont Law School, and to Virginia Church of Enfield, New Hampshire, who typed the final draft.

1

Introduction

Ever since the remote day when human beings began to
live together in society, official organs of the state have
been charged with the responsbility of deciding disputes
between individuals who belong to the community (or
are at all events temporarily within it) as well as disputes
between individuals and the state. From the beginning
of social time there have been institutions like courts
which have generated or excreted law or something
like law. In all societies beyond the most primitive a
professional class of lawyers and judges has emerged
and maintained itself. In most societies at most periods
the legal profession has been heartily disliked by all
non-lawyers: a recurrent dream of social reformers has
been that the law should be (and can be) simplified and
purified in such a way that the class of lawyers can be
done away with. The dream has never withstood the
cold light of waking reality.

Thus there has always been law and there have always
been lawyers. If we are invited to think about the growth
of the law within any society over a period of time, we
assume, instinctively, that the growth must have been
gradual, progressive, and, in some sense of the word,
rational. Our instinctive assumption is wrong with respect to most societies throughout most of recorded

history. If we think only of the common law of England and its adaptation in the North American colonies which became the United States, the assumption will still be wrong unless we take as our starting point the eighteenth century (in England) and the establishment of the federal republic in this country.

We know much less about the history of the common law than, for a long time, we thought we did. We are only beginning to learn something about the confused and chaotic process which led to its eventual emergence. An English scholar has admirably summed up this extraordinary development:

> How can a system of law, a system of ideas whose hypothesis it is that rules are constant, adapt itself to a changing world? It has not been the ordered development of the jurist or the legislator, of men thinking about law for its own sake. It has been the rough free enterprise in argument of practitioners thinking about nothing beyond the immediate interest of each client; and the strength of the system has been in the doggedness, always insensitive and often unscrupulous, with which ideas have been used as weapons. . . . The life of the common law has been in the unceasing abuse of its elementary ideas.[1]

The mindless, unconscious process which Professor Milsom graphically describes did, in the end, lead to the flowering of a distinctively English law—distinctive not so much for its substance as for its technique and style of adjudication. We do not know why this should have happened. Many societies have endured as long, or longer, without having produced anything comparable.

But in England the royal courts, which had reluctantly assumed the jurisdiction abandoned by the local and ecclesiastical courts, had, by the sixteenth century, begun to produce the raw materials from which, in time, a coherent body of law could be put together.

From the seventeenth century on, abridgments, digests, and collections of cases began to appear in England—efforts to bring some sort of order to the accumulating chaos of the case law. These were modest or low-level intellectual enterprises. Lawyers continued to think of themselves, as they were thought of by others, as being plumbers or repairmen. The law books were essentially plumbers' manuals.

II

The idea that there should or could be such a thing as a generalized theory of the common law dates from the second half of the eighteenth century. Blackstone had no predecessors. By the end of the century, lawyers had put aside their plumbers' image and become philosophers—an upgrading of status which the legal mind naturally found irresistible. Indeed, we became students not merely of law but, much more grandly, of jurisprudence—an old word wrenched into a new meaning.[2]

The eighteenth century invented not only law or jurisprudence but also history, economics, and sociology—that is, the whole range of what came to be called the social sciences.[3] No doubt, the availability of a sufficient number of case reports was a precondition to the establishment of law as a proper subject for theoretical study. But the invention or discovery of history, economics, and sociology did not in any sense depend on a specialized body of materials like our case reports. Evidently the hypothesis which commended itself to many eighteenth-century minds was that the ideas and techniques which had proved spectacularly successful in the investigation of physical phenomena could, with equal success, be applied to the investigation of social phenomena. Scientific inquiry, as the eighteenth century understood the concept, started from the assumption that there are, in whatever may be the subject matter of the investigation, observable regularities which can be identified, described, analyzed, and understood. Once that has been done, the future course of events can be predicted. And once we know what results follow from what causes, we are in a position to control, as well as to predict, the future. Extraordinary advances had been achieved in the natural sciences. The hypothesis that there are also observable regularities in the development of human societies must have been as obvious as it was attractive. Many remarkable minds set out, almost at the same time, to discover the laws of history, the laws of social and economic behavior, the laws, we might say, of law.

The eighteenth century, with good reason, thought well of itself. It was the Age of Enlightenment. It was also an age of enthusiasm and of a generally shared belief in the inevitability of progress—a belief which sustained itself throughout the nineteenth century and into our own. This pervasively optimistic intellectual ambience guaranteed that the laws which the prototypical social scientists might discover would be laws we could be proud of and live with happily, not laws which would bring us crashing down in a hopeless despair at the human condition.

We could not have developed any theories about law before the eighteenth century. The theories which were developed naturally bore the stamp of the age in which they were first hammered out. They purported to be scientific and, at the same time, assumed that everything was—or soon would be—for the best in the best of all possible worlds. Over the past two hundred years these attitudes have done a great deal to color, cloud, or distort thinking about law in successive generations.

Blackstone's celebration of the common law of England glorified the past: without quite knowing what we were about, he said, we have somehow achieved the perfection of reason. Let us preserve, unchanged, the estate which we have been lucky enough to inherit. Let us avoid any attempt at reform—either legislative or judicial—since the attempt to make incidental changes in an already perfect system can lead only to harm in ways which will be beyond the comprehension of even the most well-meaning and far-sighted innovators.[4]

Blackstone wrote at a time when English law was going through a period of rapid, violent change. Indeed, the Blackstonian construct may well be taken as a conservative reaction to the fundamental changes which the English judges were making in the apparently settled rules of English law. Using the tools of eighteenth-century analytical "philosophy," Blackstone was in effect constructing a dike which, it could be hoped, would hold back the encroaching tide. (The use of revolutionary means to achieve a conservative end is a commonplace in the intellectual history of all societies.) And the important thing about the *Commentaries* is not that an obscure lecturer at Oxford wrote them, but that, for more than a hundred years, thousands upon thousands of lawyers and influential laymen on both sides of the Atlantic read them and believed them.

The reason for the dramatic change in English law

during the second half of the eighteenth century is not far to seek. We know it as the industrial revolution. Novel methods of production and distribution required that large portions of the substantive law be rewritten in each newly industrialized country—first of all in England. Almost overnight there emerged, as independent fields of law, such commercial specialties as the law of negotiable instruments (which reflected the problems of payment and credit extension generated by the vastly increased number of mercantile transactions) and the law of sales of goods (which reflected the problems of large-scale manufacture and of distribution in markets where sellers and buyers could no longer deal face-to-face). There had, of course, been cases about bills of exchange and promissory notes, as there had been cases about sales of goods, before 1750. But there is all the difference in the world between issues which arise in litigation infrequently and irregularly (where the results are of interest only to the parties litigant) and issues which arise recurrently and regularly (where it becomes of the greatest importance to lawyers and their clients to have some idea of what the law is—or, which is even more important, what it is becoming). In that sense it is only after 1750 that it becomes possible to speak of a law of negotiable instruments and a law of sales of goods. Later entries in the fields of law which the industrial revolution bequeathed us were the law of insurance, the law of secured transactions (initially chattel mortgages, pledges, and a few conditional sales), and, of course, the law of corporations.

As anyone who has the slightest familiarity with late eighteenth-century English case law knows, the judges were quite consciously aware of what they were doing:

they were making law, new law, with a sort of joyous frenzy. Lord Mansfield was, in the eyes of his contemporaries as in those of his successors, the greatest judge of the period.[5] In one of his celebrated cases Mansfield had occasion to deal with the idea that, in English law, a contractual promise is not binding on the promisor unless it is supported by something called consideration. (At the time Mansfield decided the case, the term *consideration* had been in use in English case law for a couple of hundred years but had never acquired any precise meaning.) Mansfield's method of dealing with the problem was characteristically brutal: he abolished the consideration doctrine (whatever the doctrine may have been), at least (according to the report of the case) "in commercial cases among merchants" where the defendant's promise had been given in writing. One of Mansfield's colleagues, in his own opinion in the same case, after a lengthy review of the consideration doctrine, remarked: "Many of the old cases are strange and absurd: so also are some of the modern ones. . . ."[6] In Lord Mansfield's court the judges were not true Blackstonian believers.

We might say, making use of a famous eighteenth-century formulation, that in its own time the Blackstonian thesis (which represented what the conservative establishment wanted the law to be) was confronted with its Mansfieldian antithesis (which represented what the courts were actually doing with the law during a period of extraordinary change). The resultant nineteenth-century synthesis (at the moment we are talking only of later developments in England itself) came out muddy and blurred (which is perhaps in the nature of syntheses) but with the Blackstonian elements on

the whole in the ascendant. Many of Mansfield's most
original contributions to the developing law of trade
and commerce (and in particular his attempt to abolish
the consideration doctrine) had, within a generation
of his death, been rejected, flatly overruled or simply forgotten.[7]

III

In the preceding sections, the implicit assumption
has been that the "beginnings" of American law are
to be counted from 1800 or thereabouts. That seems
to pass over, with cavalier disregard, the nearly two
hundred years of our colonial history.

The development of our legal institutions during
those two centuries, which makes a fascinating story,
is, for a variety of reasons, irrelevant to our discussion.[8]

The law of the primitive agricultural settlements
which were painfully hacked from the wilderness in
the seventeenth century—indeed, the law of the west-
ering frontier until the conquest of the continent had
been completed—had no more relevance to the law
of our own industrialized society than the law of the
Sioux or the Cheyennes. It is true that, as the colonies
prospered and their populations multiplied, courts were
instituted and a professional class of lawyers and
judges emerged. Even so, it is pointless to speak of
an "American law" before the 1800s.

Throughout most of the eighteenth century the deep-
ening crisis in the relationship of the colonies with
England meant that our dawning national will and
energy were principally focused on evading the clear
mandate of the positive law. The function of colonial
juries was to acquit smugglers and other violators of

the Trade and Navigation Acts. The strategy of the English government was to remove litigation to the juryless forum of the vice-admiralty courts, whose judges were appointed by the Crown. It is unlikely that a struggle for national liberation ever produces a climate which is favorable to the development of a stable legal system.

In any case, there can hardly be a legal system until the decisions of the courts are regularly published and are available to bench and bar. Even in the seaboard colonies, where the practice of law had, during the eighteenth century, become professionalized, there were no published reports;[9] consequently there was nothing which could rationally be called a legal system.

With the successful issue of the Revolution and the establishment of a centralized federal government (the degree of centralization that was intended or would be achieved was, and long remained, obscure) the stage was set for a fresh start—a fresh start in the building of political institutions, in the choice of the role which government was to play in the development of our society, in the provision of a system of law for the federal republic and its constituent states. It is entirely clear that the men who guided our affairs from the 1770s or 1780s until the 1820s or 1830s understood their unique and privileged historical situation: it does not fall to the lot of every generation to make such a fresh start in a vigorous, literate, and sophisticated society already in full flood of economic and social development, conscious of its immense potential for ever-growing power and wealth.

The fact that American law dates from the end of the eighteenth century has served to differentiate our legal system not only from that of England but from those of the Western European countries with which we share a common intellectual tradition. We never experienced the mindless process of secular growth which characterized the reemergence of legal systems in England and Western Europe after the anarchy of the Dark Ages. We sloughed off our two hundred years of colonial tutelage as if they had never been. The post-Revolutionary generation of American lawyers approached the problem of providing a new law for a new land as convinced eighteenth-century rationalists, as "philosophers" in the tradition of Voltaire, Diderot, and Montesquieu.

American law has, from its late eighteenth-century beginnings, been self-conciously and self-critically aware of itself as a system which is supposed to make some kind of overall sense. It has never been allowed to grow in the chaotic, disorganized, unplanned, eccentric confusion which, even after Blackstone, continued to mark the growth of English law. American lawyers are and always have been rationalizers, generalizers, theorists—metaphysicians, we might say, *manqués*. Our theory of precedent, for example, came to be much stricter than its English analogue. In English courts which sit in panels each judge delivers his own opinion, and the opinion of each judge who votes with the majority is as authoritative as each of the other majority opinions. Thus there are usually several versions of what an English case is supposed to mean—which frees the system up considerably. American practice early came to be that one judge writes "the opinion of the court" and his opinion contains the only authoritative statement of the case.[10] I think it is also true that the American formulation of a legal rule has always tended to be more rigid, more abstract, more universal, than the English formulation. The result has been that, particularly during periods when we have taken our precedents and our theories seriously, we have had much more trouble than the English have ever had in adjusting to changing conditions. It is not altogether fanciful to link these characteristics of the American approach to law to the fact that our system was, from the beginning, consciously designed as a sort of formal garden instead of being allowed to come up as it might from the compost heap of the centuries. Our English cousins have been the romantics of the law. We have been—at least we have tried to be—the classicists.

IV

In the following chapters I shall describe the course of American law from the early 1800s until the present and set out some hypotheses on why the changes which have occurred should have occurred when they did and as they did. It is hardly necessary to say that my own version of what happened and why it should have happened will be disputed by many respectable lawyers and historians.

I have adopted a tripartite division of our legal past which was, so far as I know, first put forward by the late Karl Llewellyn, whose last book, *The Common Law Tradition*, published in 1960, was principally devoted to what he called his "periodization" of American law.[11] Llewellyn's three "periods" run from, roughly, 1800 until the Civil War; from the Civil War until World War I; from World War I until the present (or, at all events, the recent past).

Llewellyn's book seems to be largely unread, but

a great many people (either following him or having
come independently to the same conclusion) have accepted the idea that there was one fundamental change
—or mutation—in the American approach to law at
about the time of the Civil War and another at about
the time of World War I.[12] There has even developed
a consensus on what the first two periods were like.
The pre–Civil War period was our Golden Age. For
Llewellyn this was the period of what he called the
Grand Style: "style," in Llewellyn's lexicon, had nothing
to do with literary felicity or its absence but referred
to the process of adjudication—the way in which
courts go about deciding cases. After the Civil War
all the gold, by a sort of reverse alchemy, was trans-
muted into lead. The pre–Civil War Grand Style lost
out to a Formal Style, which was as bad a way of
deciding cases as the previous way had been good.

After World War I the formalistic approach which
had been dominant in American legal thought for
fifty years, went into a protracted period of breakdown and dissolution. There appears to be a general
agreement that a principal feature of the new approach,
which became manifest during the 1920s, was a root-
and-branch rejection of the formalism or (in a term
which came to have a wide vogue) the conceptualism
of the preceding period.[13] There has been, not sur-
prisingly, much less agreement about the positive accomplishments (if indeed there have been any) of the
last fifty years.

Llewellyn had persuaded himself that, during his own
professional lifetime, the pre–Civil War Grand Style
had reemerged and had once again become dominant.
He also seems to have thought that the pre–World

War I Formal Style could be dismissed as a temporary
aberration which would not (or at least need not) return.
In that optimistic assessment he has had no followers.
One approach which has enjoyed a considerable vogue
in recent years links nineteenth-century legal formalism
with nineteenth-century laissez-faire economics and the
decline of formalism with the transition to the twentieth-
century welfare state. A writer's attitude toward the
welfare state determines his view of whether the law
has been changing for the better or for the worse. What
might be called the social science approach has also had
its fervent advocates: that the law will change (or has
been changing) for the better to the extent that the legal
profession adopts (or has adopted) the theoretical insights and investigative techniques which have been
developed by the social scientists, particularly the sociologists. My own approach will become evident as the
discussion proceeds.

The discussion which follows will be largely concerned with legal doctrine as elaborated in judicial
decisions and in law books. For two or three generations
past it has been the merest truism, in much American
legal writing, that the doctrine which may be found
enshrined in case report and treatise is neither important
nor relevant. The decisions made by courts, particularly
by appellate courts, in the relatively few cases which
come into litigation and are appealed are insignificant
when they are compared with the decisions made by
legislatures, by administrative agencies, and by the
people who control large business enterprises. Therefore,
the argument runs, a study of what the courts do (or of
what the law professors say the courts do) is a great
waste of time. The only thing that is worth studying is

how decisions are made by the decision-makers who really count, among whom courts and commentators are no longer numbered.

The decisions which most dramatically affect the life of any society are not and never have been made by courts—decisions to make war (or peace), to abolish (or establish) a regime based on the private ownership of property, to enslave (or set free) all the members of a given race, to overthrow an existing government and replace it with a radically different one. These are political decisions, wise or foolish, virtuous or wicked. They have nothing to do with the concept of law, in any of the bewildering number of diverse senses in which that three-letter word is used. The need (or the opportunity) to make fundamental changes in the organization of a society occurs only at rare intervals. Most of the time we live according to established rules which will not be drawn into question until the next period of revolutionary ferment arrives. But even during periods when no one challenges the basic rules, the society we live in continues to evolve and change—in response to technological developments, to shifts in patterns of moral or religious belief, to the growth or decline of population, and so on. The process by which a society accommodates to change without abandoning its fundamental structure is what we mean by law.

In the early part of this century it was customary to draw a sharp distinction between the judicial function and the legislative function. Courts decided cases in the light of preexisting common law or statutory rules. Only the legislature could change the rules; when the legislature had spoken, the courts were bound to carry out the legislative command. We have come to see that such a distinction is not, and never was, tenable. Courts, as Justice Holmes reminded us more than half a century ago, do and must legislate—that is, change the rules to reflect the changing conditions of life.[14] And with the progressive codification of the substantive law in this century, a significant proportion of the legislative product has come to be merely a restatement of the pre-statutory common law rules—a reworking of the judicial product designed to achieve greater simplicity and clarity.

The importance of the role which the courts have played in determining social and economic policy has varied throughout our history. Until the Civil War the legislatures, state and federal, did very little; the judges, by default, took over the task of answering the questions which someone had to answer. After the Civil War the legislatures became more active; the first administrative agencies were set up toward the end of the nineteenth century. It was also during the post–Civil War period that the idea that courts never legislate—that the judicial function is merely to declare the law that already exists—became an article of faith, for lawyers and non-lawyers alike. By the 1930s, with the prodigious legislative and regulatory effort which marked the New Deal period, it became fashionable to say that the judges had had their day, which would not come again. Nevertheless, since the end of World War II we have witnessed an extraordinary resurgence of judicial activism. The anti-judicialists of the 1930s were evidently premature in consigning the courts to the dustbin of history.

The judicial product and the literature that is based on it have played and continue to play a significant part in the evolution of our society, not only during activist periods like the present but during passive periods like the one that followed the Civil War. Furthermore, the body of doctrinal material which we shall deal with has the great virtue of being available, usable, and manageable. We may concede the obvious point that legislatures, administrative agencies, and large corporations make important decisions which affect us all and which have a great deal to do with the development of our law. It does not, however, follow that much light can be shed on, say, the process of corporate decision-making by interrogating the responsible executives. They are not trained to think that way; most of the time they will have no idea how or why they arrived at a decision; if they do know, they will not necessarily be inclined to make full disclosure to an officious intermeddler. Judges are trained to explain the reasons for their decisions. They may not always be successful, but the opinions of our better judges set a model for rational and humane discourse which the rest of us can only envy.

All generalizations are oversimplifications. It is not true that, during a given fifty-year period, all the lawyers and all the judges are lighthearted innovators, joyful anarchists, and adepts of Llewellyn's Grand Style—only to be converted en masse during the next fifty-year period to formalism or conceptualism. There are formalists during innovative periods and innovators during formalistic periods—just as there are frustrated classicists during romantic periods and frustrated romantics during classical periods. When we reconstruct the past, we think we see that in one period the innovative impulse was dominant and that in another period the formalistic impulse was dominant. We are talking about temporary swings in a continuing struggle of evenly matched forces.

Within the legal profession most practicing lawyers (who are interested in winning cases or in advising their clients in such a way that they don't have cases) prefer a formalistic approach to law. That approach holds out the promise of stability, certainty, and predictability— qualities which practitioners value highly. Judges, on the other hand, are paid to decide cases. Apart from such practices as bribery and corruption (which at times become institutionalized), judges want to decide the cases which come before them sensibly, wisely, even justly. Sense, wisdom, and justice are community values, which change as the community changes. It is a reasonable assumption that swings toward or away from legal formalism are determined by changes in community values and that such swings will be more marked in the case of the judiciary than in the case of the practicing bar.

For the past hundred years academic lawyers have constituted a third distinct segment of the profession. Professors who regularly engage in practice have disappeared from the faculties of our major law schools. (Consultation work at high fees plays the same role in academia that bribery and corruption play in the courts and, like bribery and corruption, occasionally becomes institutionalized.) Most law professors spend most of their time teaching; a few of them also write books and law review articles, whose production has for a long time been an almost exclusively academic monopoly. The academic lawyers who choose to write as well as teach lack the salutary discipline which is imposed on judges who must decide (or at least appear to decide) their cases in the light of the evidence properly introduced before them in adversary proceedings. The author of a leading article in a law review need not fear being reversed on appeal: there is no higher court. The academic legal literature which has been produced over the past hundred years shows, even more dramatically than the judicial opinions of the same period, the periodic swings toward and away from formalism. It is, however, also true that a considerable number of quirky eccentrics end up teaching law and writing law books. These are people who instinctively deny what everyone else affirms. Thus, at any given time, the literature contains a considerable amount of writing which cuts against the prevailing grain. Nevertheless, the academic literature, viewed historically, brings us as close as we are apt to come to what Justice Holmes once referred to as "the felt necessities of the time."[15]

2

The Age of Discovery

I

English law was the only law that post-Revolutionary American lawyers knew anything about. A few had studied law in England. Most had received whatever training they had in this country—by serving as apprentices in law offices or by studying at the law schools which began to spring up toward the end of the eighteenth century. But the only available sources were English sources—from the crabbed and incomprehensible pages of Coke on Littleton to the elegant superficialities of Blackstone. Collections of English cases enjoyed a wide sale—either imported from London or republished here with (as time went on) "American annotations" added. There were no treatises on American law; there were no published collections of American case reports.[1]

However conscious American lawyers may have been of the need to make a fresh start, a system of law cannot be improvised overnight. It has to come from somewhere. Conceivably the European civil law systems, more or less vaguely derived from Roman law, could have been looked to for guidance, but few American lawyers had any familiarity with the civilian literature, available for the most part only in such outlandish languages as French, German, and Latin. (If the Na-

poleonic codification of French law had come a generation earlier than it did, or our own Revolution a
generation later, American law might well have borrowed liberally from the French codes—but, except
in Louisiana, the timing was wrong.)[2]

American law had to be based on English law—in
some sense and to some degree. The questions which
had to be initially decided were; In what sense? and
To what degree? Was the common law to be taken
over lock, stock, and barrel, subject to subsequent
change at the hands of American courts? Or was the
common law, along with a few statutes, to be imported
selectively—with the English rules entitled to recognition as American rules only when adopted in American
cases by American courts? And were pre-Revolutionary
English cases, and for that matter post-Revolutionary
English cases, still authoritative in American courts?
Or, if not authoritative, at least persuasive?

Such questions never received neat and tidy answers.
They could have been answered at the time the federal
Constitution was drawn up but were not. It has been
argued that the intent of the framers of the Constitution was to commit to the federal Congress and the
federal judiciary the responsibility for determining most
substantive law questions.[3] A part was to be reserved
to state courts (and legislatures) only with respect to
essentially local questions—such as title to real property. Under that approach the answers to the questions of in what sense and to what degree English law
(past and present) was to be brought over would
shortly have been provided by the Supreme Court of
the United States. However, the intent of the framers
(if that had been their intent) was never carried out

and, within a generation of the constitutional debates, was lost from memory. The accepted dogma came to be that the federal government was (and had been intended to be) a government of limited powers (with all other powers reserved to the states) and that, with respect to judicial competence, there was no "common law of the United States"—only a common law as declared by the courts of the states without review by the federal courts.[4] I shall presently have something to say about the considerable degree to which, despite the dogma, the common law was effectively federalized. However, the constitutional settlement which had been agreed to by the early 1800s precluded the simplest, and arguably most rational, solution of our legal problems by an overt federalization of almost the entire body of the law.

Thus, without constitutional guidance, the courts, state and federal, set out as joint venturers in quest of an American law. If the judges and lawyers had been left to themselves, they would in all probability have arrived, without delay, at a thoroughgoing English solution. There were, however, political forces at work which delayed the process of arriving at a consensus and influenced, in ways which it would be impossible to document, what the eventual consensus was to be.

The spirit of the frontier was hostile to the idea of a court system staffed by professionally trained judges in which clients would be represented by professionally trained lawyers. And at the time of the Revolution and for a generation after, the western parts of such states as New York and Pennsylvania were still frontier areas, albeit areas which were growing rapidly in population and political power. The people who moved restlessly westward must have been in large part those who were impatient with the constraints of a settled society. The romantic idea of a simple and natural justice, stripped of all legal artifice, is always an attractive one; during the brief periods of frontier simplicity it no doubt seemed capable of realization. The institution of lay judges was popular throughout the country; even in New York the members of the state senate (whatever their legal qualifications may have been) sat with the judges on the state's highest court of appeal until 1846. In Western states anyone who was a citizen and over twenty-one could practice law; the Abraham Lincoln bar, so-called, survived into this century.[5]

The Revolutionary trauma had instilled in many, perhaps in most, Americans, a hatred of England and all its ways—a state of mind which the untoward events which culminated in the War of 1812 prolonged for a generation after it might otherwise have disappeared. The prevalent Anglophobia led to statutes which prohibited the use of English legal materials in court proceedings, and such statutes were not restricted to the new states beyond the mountains. A New Jersey statute, enacted in 1799 and not repealed until 1819, forbade the citation not only of any English case decided later than July 4, 1776, but also (apparently without limitation of time) of "any [English] compilation, commentary, digest, lecture, treatise, or other explanation or exposition of the common law. . . ."[6] Even in states which did not go to the New Jersey extreme, it was, we may confidently assume, the part of professional wisdom for both judges and counsel to avoid, in their opinions and arguments, anything that might look like undue deference toward the common law of England.

In time both frontier romanticism and English-baiting lost their hold on the popular imagination. The law was returned to, or recaptured by, the lawyers—a process which seems to have been completed, at least in the older states, by 1820 or thereabouts. Thus the professionalization of American law was carried out not immediately after the Revolution but twenty or thirty or forty years later. The timing proved to be important in more than one way.

By 1820 a substantial body of American legal materials had accumulated. The decisions of American courts, state and federal, were being published. Books on American law were beginning to appear as well as American republications (with added local annotations) of English books and case collections. There was an indigenous base for an American law which had not existed a generation earlier. The only professional solution which can be imagined, as of the 1780s, would have been a total borrowing of English law, which would then have been adapted, bit by bit and piece by piece, to fit the conditions of American life. In the 1820s such a total borrowing was no longer necessary. We had our own cases. Our courts were long-established institutions. American judges—Marshall and Story on the Supreme Court of the United States, Chancellor Kent in New York, and others—enjoyed a well-merited prestige. We no longer needed the totality of English law, although, with the abatement of anti-English feeling, we could profitably borrow from the inexhaustible storehouse of the English case law (including the current English cases).

Another consequence of the enforced delay in settling on the bases of our legal system was that we could look to English law, particularly the law relating to trade and commerce, as that law had been reshaped, or invented, by Lord Mansfield and his colleagues. In England itself the tide was already beginning to turn against Mansfield: his radical approach to the problem of judicial law-making was in course of being scrapped in favor of a quasi-Blackstonian approach which emphasized adherence to precedent.[7] In this country, however, a pure Mansfieldianism flourished: not only were his cases regularly cited but his lighthearted disregard for precedent, his joyous acceptance of the idea that judges are supposed to make law—the more law the better—became a notable feature of our early jurisprudence. Justice Story, in particular, both in his opinions and in his non-judicial writings, never tired of acknowledging his indebtedness to, and his reverence for, Lord Mansfield.

The fact that we did not seriously set about building an American legal system until well after 1800 also meant that the society for which the law was being provided was no longer the agricultural society which Thomas Jefferson had hoped would be our permanent state. By the 1820s the process of industrialization was far advanced. The profound shock of technological change was already being experienced, as the eighteenth-century world of stagecoaches and cottage manufacture was metamorphosed into the new and unsettling world of railroads and factories. The problems which our industrializing society faced in the 1820s were not unlike those which the English courts had dealt with fifty or seventy-five years earlier—which may have been a factor in our enthusiastic acceptance of Mansfieldianism.

Finally, the delay meant that the task of building a legal system had to be approached in the light of the constitutional settlement which had apparently denied to the federal government and the federal courts the power to insure that our emerging law would be nationally uniform, to the extent that national uniformity was, as to some degree it obviously was, essential. The danger of a state-by-state fragmentation of the substantive law became a matter of concern to many observers.[8] Some way had to be found of achieving the national uniformity which the received constitutional dogma seemed to make impossible. Indeed, the quest for uniformity has ever since remained one of our most urgent goals of law reform. With what may be the American genius for steering a middle course between extremes, the quest has never been entirely successful but the dangers of fragmentation have never been entirely realized either. The course of our legal development has been decisively influenced by the shifting fortunes of this continuing struggle. During the pre–Civil War period the proponents of national uniformity—who were never a coherently organized group—seem to have hit on several courses of action, all of which, even though they may appear to have been mutually inconsistent, were diligently pursued.

II

The first national uniformity proposal which was seriously put forward was a call for a general codification of the law.[9] In England, Jeremy Bentham had been the first advocate of codification, although he was a prophet without honor in his own country.[10] So far as we can tell, Bentham had no great influence in this

country either. Bentham himself, in 1811, had proposed
to President Madison the project of a comprehensive
federal code, with Bentham as the draftsman. Madison,
who had other matters to preoccupy him, did not take
up the offer. There is no reason why Bentham should
have been familiar with current developments in American constitutional law, but, even at the time when he
composed his letter to Madison, a federal codification
was no longer a political possibility: that debate was
over and done with.

The movement in favor of codification at the state
level—a proposal which was eloquently supported by
Justice Story as early as 1821—was not Benthamite
either in its inspiration or in its detail.[11] For Story and
others, codification seemed to be the most promising
way—perhaps the only way—of dealing with the problem posed by the mounting flood of case reports
(already, at that early date, felt to be unmanageable) as
well as with the problem of a substantive law fragmented
into as many subdivisions as there were states (with the
number of new states increasing decade by decade).
It was assumed, and the assumption may well have
been correct, that if a leading state—New York or
Massachusetts, for example—codified its law, the other
states would adopt the New York or Massachusetts
Code and in that way the law would become uniform
throughout the country. Furthermore, in Story's
peculiarly American version of the codification idea,
what was needed was not a universal codification—such
a project, Story once commented, would be "positively
mischievous, or inefficacious, or futile"—but a limited
one, restricted to fields of law which had achieved
maturity, stability, and a general acceptance (he sug-

gested "commercial contracts" as an example of what he had in mind).[12] It is true that David Dudley Field, who became the leader of the New York codification movement and who had been influenced not only by the French codes but also, quite possibly, by Bentham, had a much more ambitious vision of codification than Story ever had.[13]

Since the pre-Civil War codification movement ultimately failed—after having come within a hair's breadth of success in New York—we tend to underestimate the influence which it exerted for the better part of half a century. The codification idea had a large popular following for reasons which had nothing to do with the sophisticated theories of professionals like Story and Field. The codifiers did not think of themselves as idealistic reformers dedicated to a lost cause. They were practical men who had caught hold of a good idea whose time had, as they and many others felt, come. From the 1820s until the Civil War, American lawyers lived with the idea that the common law not only could be but probably would be codified—that the general principles which underlay the cases, in their hundreds and their thousands, could be and probably would be set out in a connected series of reasoned propositions. That way of thinking about the law no doubt contributed to the extraordinary flexibility—the open-endedness—which became a characteristic of American law during this period.

The national uniformity idea, which had been one of the motivating forces behind the codification movement, expressed itself, in a different guise, through the early provision of a specifically American legal literature. If the law could not be unified by the enactment of uniform statutes—or codes—throughout the country, perhaps it could be unified through an authoritative formulation in learned treatises. Nothing comparable to the American treatises which soon appeared in profusion had, at that time, been seen in England. Chancellor Kent's significantly entitled *Commentaries on American Law*—originally lectures which he had given at Columbia College beginning in 1823, following his retirement from the bench—were published between 1826 and 1830 and enjoyed a fabulous (although, in my own opinion, unmerited) success: as late as 1872 they appeared in a twelfth edition, edited by a recent graduate of the Harvard Law School named Oliver Wendell Holmes, Jr.[14] Beginning in 1831 Justice Story moonlighted as Dane Professor of Law at Harvard and, by the time of his death in 1845, had produced nine major treatises and had planned to begin work on a tenth— on admiralty—the following year.[15] The Story treatises, like Kent's *Commentaries*, were quite consciously designed to lay the foundations for an American law derived from but in no sense confined by the principles of English law. The treatises, unlike the *Commentaries*, were works of impressive scholarship and of great originality. Nothing like them, in English, had ever been seen before; for the better part of a hundred years no books of comparable excellence were produced in any English-speaking country. The Story treatises remained in print as late as the 1900s; their vogue and their authority were by no means restricted to this country. Story's remarkable powers of analysis have been obscured by a style which, for twentieth-century tastes, is one of intolerable prolixity. Any reader who can adjust himself to the stylistic conventions of the first half of the nineteenth century will find a great deal to admire, even to marvel at, in Story's thousands of pages.

There was evidently money to be made writing—or, at all events, publishing—law books. Following the great success of Kent and Story, a professional class of law-book writers emerged. For the most part these writers were not academics nor were they distinguished practitioners or judges. They were hacks who would run up a book on negotiable instruments this year, a book on corporations next year, and a book on insurance the year after that. The books were conceived as manuals for practitioners and were mostly uncritical collections of case digests. The best of them, however, were astonishingly good and, until the West Publishing Company established the National Reporter System in the 1880s, they were the essential stock-in-trade of the working lawyer.[16]

By the time of the Civil War a comprehensive legal literature, specifically directed to American doctrines and American developments, had been provided. It was a literature which, apart from such exceptional accomplishments as Story's, had no jurisprudential pretensions whatever. And yet, even the dreariest hack does, to some extent, organize his material, does impose an orderly sequence, does try to make sense of what is going on. The first flowering of our legal literature contributed greatly to the continuing struggle to keep an American law in being.

Even though the idea of a wholesale federalization of the substantive law was rejected at an early stage, the Supreme Court of the United States has, throughout our history, discovered and exploited various methods of establishing federal supremacy—and thus national uniformity.

One of these methods has been to give an expansive reading to the powers conferred by the Constitution on the federal government and the federal courts. The most dramatic example of this process during the pre-Civil War period was the Supreme Court's progressive expansion of the admiralty jurisdiction ambiguously conferred on the federal courts by Section 2 of Article III.[17] The constitutional grant covered "all causes of admiralty and maritime jurisdiction." By the time of the Civil War the Supreme Court had completed the process of construing that provision to mean that, with a few whimsical exceptions, federal law governed all aspects of the shipping industry and extended, territorially, to the inland lakes and rivers as well as to the coastal waters and the high seas. The Court's construction of the "admiralty and maritime jurisdiction" clause becomes more interesting when it is understood that the entire history of admiralty law both in England and in the North American colonies suggested (indeed, if the history was to be taken seriously, compelled) a much, much narrower reading. Thus, by the simple expedient of paying no attention whatever to the known meaning of the words chosen by the constitutional draftsmen, the Court effectively federalized—nationalized—the law relating to all waterborne transportation.

The federalizing Supreme Court also succeeded in reversing, for all practical purposes, the outcome of the constitutional debate which had allocated control of the substantive law to the states. My reference is to the celebrated case of *Swift* v. *Tyson*, decided in 1842, with Justice Story (who had been the Court's principal

spokesman in the expansion of the admiralty jurisdiction) writing the opinion for a substantially unanimous Court.[18] The doctrine of *Swift* v. *Tyson* was
that the federal courts would exercise an independent
judgment—that is, would not be bound by the law of any
state—in questions of, as Story put it, general commercial law. All lawyers know the ignominious end
which, a hundred years later, was reserved for *Swift* v.
Tyson.[19] Most of us no longer know what the case was
about or what the doctrine which Story announced for
the Court was or how it worked. These matters will be
worth a few minutes of our time.

The case involved a technical, but by no means un-
important, point of negotiable instruments law: whether
an indorsee of a bill of exchange, who had taken it in
payment of a preexisting debt, held the bill free of
defenses available between the original parties. If the
indorsee had paid money for the bill, he would unques-
tionably have held free of the defenses. Without going
into the merits of the question, it suffices to say that no
student of negotiable instruments law, from the time
that law began to take its modern shape in the late
eighteenth century down to the present time, has ever
doubted that antecedent debt and new value should, for
this purpose, be treated as functional equivalents.

Swift v. *Tyson* came to the Supreme Court from the
federal court in New York. The defendant, Tyson, had
accepted the bill in New York City. For that reason it
was assumed that the case was governed by New York
law (if indeed the law of any state was relevant). On the
point at issue, New York law had fallen into a certain
amount of confusion. Chancellor Kent, who knew his
negotiable instruments law, had held in a case called

Coddington v. *Bay*[20] that a purchaser who had taken a
bill under suspicious circumstances and outside the
usual course of business was not protected but added
that taking a bill in payment of a debt was entirely
within the usual course of business. Kent was affirmed
on appeal to the Court of Errors (which was then the
highest court in the state). However, careless language
in the opinion in the Court of Errors apparently misled
some lower court judges, with the result that there were
a couple of recent (as of 1842) lower court decisions
which had got the preexisting debt question wrong.

It is always a matter of great interest when a sophisticated court chooses to ignore an obvious solution to a
simple case and instead elects to use the case as a
vehicle for making an important doctrinal pronounce-
ment. The obvious solution to *Swift* v. *Tyson* was to
have pointed out that the only authoritative statement
of New York law on the preexisting debt question had
been by Chancellor Kent in *Coddington* v. *Bay* (as well
as in his *Commentaries*). Careless dicta in the Court of
Errors and the subsequent confusion of a few lower
court judges were entitled to no weight. Thus the law
of New York coincided with that of the rest of the
civilized world and there was no need to go any further.
Story's opinion makes it entirely clear that he understood the point. Therefore the conclusion is inescapable
that he and his colleagues had decided to use this
ridiculous case as the opportunity for federalizing—or
nationalizing—a large part of the common law of the
United States. Indeed, the arguments of counsel, which
are summarized at length in the report, reinforce that
conclusion. Mr. Dana, technically the losing counsel,
made a brilliant argument in which, in effect, he gave

aid and comfort to his nominal adversary, Mr. Fessenden. Neither Dana nor Fessenden even pretended to take the New York cases seriously. Perhaps the truth was that *Swift* v. *Tyson* was a made up case in which everyone concerned had agreed that the minor confusion in the New York law of negotiable instruments provided an admirable opportunity for inviting the Supreme Court of the United States to take a great leap forward toward the goal of a nationally uniform law.

Story's uncharacteristically brief opinion was a masterpiece of disingenuousness. He would have had the reader believe that the interesting question of whether the federal courts were bound by state rules of decisional law—technically a question of construction of the Rules of Decision Act of 1789—had never before occurred to him or his colleagues. Blandly ignoring the many available authorities which had accumulated during his own long tenure on the Court,[21] he wrapped up the argument in half a page. The answer was that federal courts should pay respectful attention to the decisions of state courts but, except for issues of essentially local interest, should decide cases in the light of general principles.[22] Indeed, Story seemed to suggest that, under the ultimate superintendence of the Supreme Court, there would be only one nationalized law in state as well as in federal courts. He closed this crucial passage with a rousing tag from Cicero to the effect that the day will come when the law will be the same in Rome and in Athens and throughout the world—*apud omnes gentes, omni tempore, una eademque lex.* He then added a magisterial review of the development of negotiable instruments law on the antecedent debt question and called it a day.

The point about *Swift* v. *Tyson* is that it was immedi-

ately and enthusiastically accepted. No one suggested
that it was an unconstitutional usurpation of power by
power-crazed judges or that it was a trick played by a
wily Federalist justice on his unsuspecting Jacksonian
colleagues. No bumper stickers called for Justice Story's
impeachment. On the contrary, the doctrine of the
general commercial law was warmly welcomed and
expansively construed, not only by the lower federal
courts but by the state courts as well.[23] For the next half
century the Supreme Court of the United States became
a great commercial law court. As novel issues generated
controversy and conflict, the court's function was to
propose a generally acceptable synthesis. The Justices,
not having been divinely inspired, did not always suc-
ceed, but in a surprising number of instances they were
able to produce solutions which promptly became the
law of the land, whatever the forum of litigation might
be.[24]

The virtues of the *Swift* v. *Tyson* idea as a device for
achieving national uniformity are obvious. Less obvious,
but, it may be, even more important, was the approach
to the process of adjudication which Story's *Swift* v.
Tyson opinion counseled. Courts, said Story, should
not take a narrow view of precedent. They should look
to the entire range of the available literature, scholarly
as well as judicial, English and European as well as
American. They should take into account the social
and economic consèquences of their decisions. Story
was preaching what would be somewhat barbarously
referred to a hundred years later as a policy-oriented
approach to law. That approach accurately reflected
the creative and innovative spirit which was a note-
worthy feature of American law during the pre–Civil

War period. The *Swift* v. *Tyson* opinion was one of the most eloquent, as it was one of the most influential, statements of what that spirit was.

A feature of the American approach to law which has always bewildered and not infrequently shocked foreign observers is that our courts routinely assume jurisdiction over issues which in most other countries are thought to lie well beyond the limits of judicial competence. Alexis de Tocqueville noticed this, and was impressed by it, in the 1830s:[25] thus the exercise of what was, by comparative standards, an extraordinary degree of judicial power was a phenomenon which had rooted itself in our practice well before the Civil War. The early assumption by the Supreme Court of the United States of the power to declare acts of Congress, as well as the acts of state legislatures and the decisions of state courts, unconstitutional was only the tip of the iceberg. From the beginning our courts, both state and federal, seem to have been willing to answer any conceivable question which any conceivable litigant might choose to ask. And from the beginning—which is even more curious— the American people, which throughout most of our history has distrusted lawyers, seems to have acquiesced in, indeed to have enthusiastically welcomed, the arrogation of unlimited power by the judges.

I assume that this distinctively American development was the unplanned result of the several aspects of our pre–Civil War history which we have been discussing. We did cut ourselves loose from the English tradition. We did set out to create a rationally organized system of law. We did have to adjust that system—somehow— to the dizzying pace of social, economic, and technological change. We did have to cope, in the real world, with the complicated problems which arose from the obscure metaphysical concept of an indissoluble union of indestructible states. The federal Congress did little; the state legislatures did less. The judges became our preferred problem-solvers.

The broad—indeed unlimited—range of issues which came to be committed to the courts for final solution added still another dimension to the American concept of law.

III

There was one issue—the issue which eventually tore the Union apart—which neither the judges nor any one else could control or deal with. The judicial contribution to the ongoing debate about slavery may have served to aggravate the situation and precipitate the catastrophe.[26]

Few people, in the modern world, have questioned the proposition that slavery is morally wrong. Whether slavery, at least under some circumstances, is economically right is a different question.[27] However, the economic rightness of slavery—say, in our Southern states during the nineteenth century—is irrelevant to what we feel (or what the people who lived then felt) about the institution itself. Let it be conceded that the use of slave labor was the best or the cheapest or the most efficient way of growing cotton. No amount of economic benefit could weigh in the balance against the universal moral condemnation of chattel slavery. An economic justification of slavery would stand on the same footing as Dean Swift's Modest Proposal for solving the chronic deficiency of meat in the Irish diet by having the Irish eat the large and unwanted surplus of babies.

The great and wicked compromise, without which there could never have been a federal union, was the recognition of slavery (a word which is never used in the Constitution) as an arrangement entitled to constitutional protection. In the 1780s, most people, both in free states and in slave states, may well have assumed that slavery would disappear in the South as it already had in the North. But, despite the abolition of the foreign slave trade in 1808, the institution flourished and even developed its own apologists; after the 1820s or 1830s the conditions of enslavement seem to have become progressively harsher and more inhumane. Nevertheless, the powers of the federal government (including the federal courts) had to be mobilized to protect the slaveholder's property, wherever that property might be found.

What is a judge to do when, in his judicial capacity, he is required to enforce a law which, as a private person, he regards as profoundly immoral? Many judges, in the South as well as in the North, confronted that dilemma. For Southern antislavery judges the problem was the institution of slavery itself, in all its ramifications. For Northern antislavery judges the problem came up mostly in proceedings under the Fugitive Slave Act to force the return of escaped slaves (or alleged slaves) to their owners.

A judge so situated has several options. He can resign his judgeship. Or he can offer himself as a candidate for impeachment by saying: I regard this law as immoral and refuse to enforce it in my court. Or he can evade the issue by seizing on minor technical lapses (usually procedural) and dismissing the case. Or he can enforce the law, with death in his heart—because it is the law, duly established by the constituted authorities, and because, as a judge, he has no other choice.

In the real world most judges follow either the route of technical evasion (which exalts procedural detail over substance) or the route of blind obedience (which exalts a sort of Platonic idea of the law over reality). Either route leads its followers to or toward a formalistic conception of law in which the purpose for which a rule of law exists is lost from sight; in which the law, which must always be looked on as a means, becomes its own end; in which the letter lives while the spirit dies.

Justice Story of the Supreme Court and Chief Justice Shaw of Massachusetts are among the notable judicial figures of the period who are known to have been convinced antislavery men. Much of this chapter testifies to Story's extraordinary contributions to the development of our law. Shaw was also one of our great judges —less erudite than Story, not a scholar on the bench but a man who enjoyed grappling with novel and difficult issues, which he did with tough-minded originality.[28] It fell to the lot of both men to write opinions in slavery cases.[29] In these opinions they seem to have been driven into a formalism which was entirely foreign to the ideas they had expressed and the principles they had stood for during their long careers.[30]

One of the hidden costs of the national agony which culminated in the Civil War may have been the crippling of our legal system. If judges like Story and Shaw were driven into formalism, so were many lesser judges. And once the tools of formalism have been used, even in a good cause, they are there, ready to hand, tempting. It is among other things extremely easy to decide cases

according to the letter of a statute or of an established
rule of law, without further inquiry. The intolerable
pressures to which even Story and Shaw succumbed may
have been responsible for the first appearance of the
techniques of formalism in our case law. Those techniques, however, had a long and brilliant future ahead
of them.[31]

IV

Karl Llewellyn once observed that what he called the
Grand Style in pre–Civil War American cases was an
unusual thing to find in the legal history of any society.
He had found no traces of such a style in any of the
other modern legal systems—principally English and
German—with which he was familiar. One of the few
periods in the past in which a comparable style had
flourished was, he suggested, the classical period of
Roman jurisprudence—roughly the third century of
our era.[32] If there is anything in the Roman law analogy,
we might hypothesize that by the third century it had
become clear that the parochial law of the city-state
which Rome had once been no longer served the needs
of a world empire. Thus in Rome in the third century, as
in the United States in the nineteenth century, a stable,
wealthy, and powerful society found both the need and
the opportunity to create a rational system of law. We
know little enough about what happened in Rome
during the third century and nothing at all about why,
after half a century, the explosion of creative energy
should have spent itself, never to be repeated, as the
Roman world stumbled toward its doom.

In our history, as in the history of Rome, the period
of glorious achievement came, almost overnight, to its

end. No golden age endures forever—even if the barbarians do not invade, even if all the slaves are freed. In the history of literature and the arts we are familiar with the phenomenon of a great creative period which vanishes as suddenly and as unexpectedly as it came— the Elizabethan theater at the end of the sixteenth century and the Viennese school of music at the end of the eighteenth are two obvious examples among many. It may be that, for reasons which escape our grasp, the best and most creative minds of a generation are drawn to a particular field—which may be the creation of a new kind of theater or of a new style of music or, as in the North American colonies after 1750, the creation of a new kind of government or, as in our federal republic after 1800, the creation of a system of law. After a generation or two of intense activity the job is done; the best and most creative minds of the next generation follow their genius into new fields. But it will be a long time before anyone realizes that the last great play has already been written, the last great symphony composed.

3

The Age of Faith

I

My description of American law before the Civil War
sounded like a romp through the Garden of Eden.
Wherever we went we paused to admire the happy sight
of great judges deciding great cases greatly, aware of
the lessons of the past but conscious of the needs of the
future, striking a sensitive balance between the conflicting claims of local automony and national uniformity in an immense, diverse, and rapidly growing
country, creating a new law for a new land. Only the
issue of slavery, which cast an ever-lengthening shadow,
disturbed the tranquillity of the scene.

When we turn to our next period—roughly from the
Civil War to World War I—we find ourselves expelled
from our lovely sunlit garden and condemned to wander
uncertainly in the law's black night. And yet American
law apparently achieved its greatest triumphs during
this period. Never had lawyers and judges and the new
breed of law professors been so confident, so self-
assured, so convinced beyond the shadow of a doubt,
that they were serving not only righteousness but truth.
Never had the idea of law as the ultimate salvation of
a free society—a government not of men but of laws—
so captured the imagination of any people. Never before
had any society taken a professional man of law—

Holmes, about whom I shall have more to say presently
—as the embodiment of its dream. Perhaps, when everyone is blind, it is child's play to persuade ourselves that
we now see better than our sighted predecessors ever
did.

Christopher Columbus Langdell, who in 1870 became
the first dean of the Harvard Law School, has long been
taken as a symbol of the new age.[1] A better symbol
could hardly be found; if Langdell had not existed, we
would have had to invent him. Langdell seems to have
been an essentially stupid man who, early in his life, hit
on one great idea to which, thereafter, he clung with all
the tenacity of genius. Langdell's idea evidently cor-
responded to the felt necessities of the time. However
absurd, however mischievous, however deeply rooted
in error it may have been, Langdell's idea shaped our
legal thinking for fifty years.

Langdell's idea was that law is a science. He once
explained how literally he took that doubtful proposition:

> [A]ll the available materials of that science [that is,
> law] are contained in printed books. . . . [T]he
> library is . . . to us all that the laboratories of the
> university are to the chemists and physicists, all
> that the museum of natural history is to the zool-
> ogists, all that the botanical garden is to the
> botanists. . . .[2]

From that basic proposition several subsidiary propositions followed.

Ideologically, it followed that legal truth is a species
of scientific truth. The quality of scientific truth, as
most nineteenth-century minds understood it, is that

once such a truth has been demonstrated, it endures. It is not subject to change without notice. It does not capriciously turn into its own opposite. It is, like the mountain, there. The jurisprudential premise of Langdell and his followers was that there is such a thing as the one true rule of law which, being discovered, will endure, without change, forever. This strange idea colored, explicitly or implicitly, all the vast literature which the Langdellians produced.

The methodological consequences of "law is a science" may have been even more fateful than the ideological consequences. Scientific advance is generally thought to consist of progressive simplification. The better the hypothesis, the more phenomena it will explain. The fewer the formulas that are needed to explain whatever it is that we are investigating, the better.

Langdell put the idea this way:

> [T]he number of fundamental legal doctrines is much less than is commonly supposed; the many different guises in which the same doctrine is constantly making its appearance, and the great extent to which legal treatises are a repetition of each other, being the cause of much misapprehension. If these doctrines could be so classified and arranged that each should be found in its proper place, and nowhere else, they would cease to be formidable from their number.[3]

The Langdellians sought, with considerable success, to formulate theories which would cover broad areas of the common law and reduce an unruly diversity to a manageable unity. Let us, by way of example, consider the development of what came to be called the law of contract.

Contract liability, as we think of it, is liability imposed on a defendant who has voluntarily undertaken some obligation which, without excuse, he has failed to perform, his unexcused failure having caused loss to (or prevented gain by) the person in whose favor the obligation runs. Historians tell us that English law for several centuries after the Norman Conquest did not recognize liability for a failure or refusal to perform a promised undertaking; liability was imposed only for a faulty attempt to perform which resulted in loss or damage (typically physical).[4] Thus I could not recover damages from a blacksmith who had promised to shoe my horse but had not done so (even if it was entirely clear that the unavailability of my horse had caused me loss). However, if the blacksmith did shoe the horse but did it in such a way that the horse came up lame, I could recover damages for the injury to the horse in an action of trespass. During the sixteenth century the courts began to impose liability for breach of a purely promissory undertaking. The new action in which I could recover damages from the blacksmith for his failure to shoe the horse at all was called assumpsit; sixteenth-century lawyers seem to have looked on assumpsit as a spin-off from an action called trespass on the case (or case), which was itself a liberalized version of the original action of trespass. (Trespass and case are looked on as the ancestors of what we call tort; assumpsit is looked on as the ancestor of what we call contract.) Assumpsit in time was subdivided into special assumpsit, general assumpsit, and indebitatus assumpsit—the details of which we need not inquire into (indeed for a hundred years only a few historians have had even the vaguest idea about what the difference between, say, special assumpsit and general assumpsit could have been). No one ever developed a theory of assumpsit. In a preindustrial society, contract liability, however it might be referred to, was not a matter of much importance: Blackstone devoted only a few pages to it.

With the industrial revolution contract liability became all important—indeed the word *contract* began to displace the word *assumpsit* in the legal vocabulary, and the first books on contracts appeared in England.[5] The first American book on contracts was not published until 1844.[6] The terminological shift from *assumpsit* to *contract* suggests, no doubt, a recognition of change. Even so, in the pre-Langdellian era, no one thought of developing a theory of contract any more than any one had ever thought of developing a theory of assumpsit. There were as many types of contracts as there were classes of people to enter into them: contracts of factors, brokers, auctioneers, executors and administrators, trustees, seamen, corporations, guardian and ward, masters of ships, guarantors, landlord and tenant—and on and on in a never-ending list.[7]

In a pluralistic age, no one saw any reason why all these types of contracts should be subjected to a unitary set of rules: each class of contractors could be left to work out arrangements appropriate to the relevant trade, business, or profession. In the early books, general theoretical discussion—the consideration doctrine, the theory of conditions, the requirement of mutual assent—was minimal or nonexistent. What counted was what real people were doing in the real world.

With the Langdellians all that changed. The key to the general theory of contract which quickly emerged was that a unitary set of rules was now to cover all possible situations.[8] The status of the contracting parties and the subject matter of their deal were no longer to be taken into account. The law, under the new dispensation, no longer recognized factors or brokers, farmers or workers, merchants or manufacturers, shipowners or railroads, husbands or wives, parents or children— only faceless characters named A and B, whoever they might be and whatever it might be they were trying to accomplish.

What happened on the contract side was duplicated on the tort side. The word *tort* itself was a new invention which, for a generation or so, was used hesitantly, along with a parenthetical explanation of what the word was supposed to mean.[9] Until the second half of the nineteenth century lawyers had not seen any need for a single word—or concept—which would cover all sorts of liability imposed for non-contractual loss, damage, or personal injury suffered by a plaintiff as the result of a defendant's wrongful acts. No one had ever thought that a unitary set of rules could (or should) be developed which would apply to trespass, case, conversion, fraud, misrepresentation, assault, and so on.[10] A general theory of torts (or wrongs) had been as foreign to the legal imagination as a general theory of assumpsit or contracts had been. But first the word and then the theory were quickly provided. As with the new theory of contracts, the new theory of torts was designed to cover all possible situations in which any A might be ordered to pay damages to any B to compensate him for personal injury or property damage, with as little account as possible being taken of who A and B were and the particular circumstances of their confrontation.

Langdell had pointed out that the law library was our laboratory and that the printed case reports were our experimental materials. It followed, therefore, that we were to study the cases and that, in our teaching, casebooks were to replace treatises. It was, however, no part of Langdell's scheme that we were to study all the cases.

> [T]he cases which are useful and necessary for [the purpose of mastering legal principles or doctrines] bear an exceedingly small proportion to all that have been reported. The vast majority are useless, worse than useless, for any purpose of systematic study.[11]

Thus the vast majority of all reported cases, past and present, are worse than useless and should be disregarded. The function of the legal scholar, whether he is writing a treatise or compiling a casebook, is to winnow out from the chaff those very few cases which have ever been correctly decided and which, if we follow them, will lead us to the truth. That is to say, the doctrine—the one true rule of law—does not in any sense emerge from the study of real cases decided in the real world. The doctrine tests the cases, not the other way around.

Langdell, in his pioneering casebook on contracts, introduced the device, which long remained in fashion, of relying almost entirely on sequences of English cases, arranged chronologically; he admitted a few sequences of New York and Massachusetts cases but no other American jurisdictions were recognized. There was no

other way in which the ideal of the one true rule of law
could have been realized. Since 1800 the principal
characteristics of American law had been its chaotic
diversity, its sensitivity to changing conditions, its
fluidity, its pluralism. All that had to be suppressed. I
might add that no American law student or lawyer or,
for that matter, judge was then, any more than now, in
a position to know whether the relatively few English
cases which the Langdellians admitted to the pantheon
of correct doctrine were in any sense representative of
what English law was or at any time in the past had
been. It is also fair to say that the Langdellians, both
in their casebooks and their treatises, performed major
surgery on what their chosen English cases had been
about when they were real cases in a real England.[12]
England became our never-never land, our Shangri-La,
our Utopia.

II

If Langdell gave the new jurisprudence its methodology, Holmes, more than any one else, gave it its
content. However, the Langdellians—the members of
the orthodox Establishment, we might say—rejected,
ignored, or perhaps simply misunderstood many aspects
of Holmes's complex thought. What they picked up and
put to their own simpleminded use was a sort of
bowdlerized, expurgated version of what Holmes had
actually said.[13]

Holmes is a strange, enigmatic figure. Put out of your
mind the picture of the tolerant aristocrat, the great
liberal, the eloquent defender of our liberties, the
Yankee from Olympus. All that was a myth, concocted
principally by Harold Laski and Felix Frankfurter,

about the time of World War I.[14] The real Holmes was savage, harsh, and cruel, a bitter and lifelong pessimist who saw in the course of human life nothing but a continuing struggle in which the rich and powerful impose their will on the poor and weak. Holmes had no use for the gentle optimism of Karl Marx who seems to have believed that after one more revolution the world would be a better place. According to Holmes:

> [T]he *ultima ratio*, not only *regum*, but of private persons, is force, and ... at the bottom of all private relations, however tempered by sympathy and all the social feelings, is a justifiable self-preference. If a man is on a plank in the deep sea which will only float one, and a stranger lays hold of it, he will thrust him off if he can. When the state finds itself in a similar position, it does the same thing.[15]

In this bleak and terrifying universe, the function of law, as Holmes saw it, is simply to channel private aggressions in an orderly, perhaps in a dignified, fashion. He reduced all of jurisprudence to a single, frightening statement:

> The first requirement of a sound body of law is, that it should correspond with the actual feelings and demands of the community, whether right or wrong.[16]

That is, if the dominant majority (which seems to be what Holmes meant by "the community") desires to persecute blacks or Jews or communists or atheists, the law, if it is to be "sound," must arrange for the persecution to be carried out with, as we might say,

due process. If the law does not adopt popular prejudices, whatever they may be, the only alternative,
Holmes went on to explain, is private—that is, extra-
legal—retribution against the despised minorities.

Holmes, in his radical and despairing pessimism, cut
against the grain of most nineteenth-century thought.
Holmes also differed from most of his contemporaries
in his understanding of the nature of scientific inquiry. Holmes by no means rejected the "law is a
science" idea, but his own ideas about the scientific
method and the qualities of scientific truth were at
a far remove from those accepted as self-evident by
most nineteenth-century minds.

Holmes's thinking may have been influenced by his
membership in a group of young men who, calling
themselves the Metaphysical Club, met regularly in
Boston and Cambridge from 1870 to 1872. William
James was one of the members. Another was a man
named Charles Peirce who, almost unknown in his
own lifetime, has since his death acquired a considerable vogue among philosophers.[17] Peirce held strik-
ingly original views both about the nature of scientific
inquiry and about the nature of knowledge. Peirce
did not look on scientific inquiry as a method of dis-
covering or revealing truth. His hypothesis was that
inquiry is a never-ending process whose purpose is to
resolve doubts generated when experience does not
mesh with preconceived theory. When the relevant
community of investigators has arrived at a consensus
which provides a new basis for belief, the unpleasant
sensation of doubt is, for a time, overcome. Peirce
emphasized not only the continuing nature of the process of inquiry but also what might be called the ob-

jective or communal nature of knowledge. These ideas
seem to correspond with the central tenets of Holmes's
jurisprudential theory. Holmes never acknowledged
any debt to Peirce or for that matter to any one else.
All we know is that, over a period of several years,
both men attended meetings of a group at which
these ideas were, in all probability, discussed.

In 1880 Holmes was approaching his fortieth year.
He apparently believed that a man who does not have
some great accomplishment to his credit before he
is forty will never accomplish anything. For the better
part of fifteen years he had been practicing law in
Boston, without great success. He had prepared an
edition of Kent's *Commentaries*[18] and had written a
number of law review articles. But the great accomplishment had eluded him. At that point he was invited
to deliver a series of lectures at the Lowell Institute
in Boston. He seems to have looked on this opportunity as his last chance to meet his own deadline for
greatness. He must have been pleased—or relieved—
at the astonishing reaction to his lectures, both when
they were delivered in November and December of
1880 and when they were published the following
spring under the title *The Common Law*. Within a
year a professorship had been established for him at
Harvard which, much to the annoyance of his new
Harvard colleagues, he almost immediately resigned
to accept an appointment to the Supreme Judicial
Court of Massachusetts. After his appointment to the
bench Holmes never returned to the world of scholarship, so that the lectures in *The Common Law* remain
as his only attempt to formulate a coherent, comprehensive statement of his theories about law.

The lectures have long since become unreadable unless the reader is prepared to put forward an almost superhuman effort of will to keep his attention from flagging and his interest from wandering. Our difficulty with the lectures may stem from the fact that they are not what they pretend to be. They pretend to be a historical survey of the development of a few fundamental common law principles which, according to Holmes, had recurrently manifested themselves in the several fields he chose to deal with—principally criminal law, torts, and contracts. In fact, the historical underpinning was patently absurd, even when it had not been deliberately distorted. I do not mean to suggest that Holmes was a poor historian or that he did not know what he was doing. He was an excellent historian and knew more about what he was doing than most of us do. He was making a highly original, essentially philosophical statement about the nature of law. For reasons which he never explained, he chose to dress his statement in the misleading disguise of pseudo-history. Perhaps the disguise was a way of sugarcoating the pill—of making the new and unfamiliar appear to be old and familiar. Perhaps it was an elaborate joke which it amused Holmes, who was of a sardonic turn of mind, to play on his audience.[19]

Our difficulty with the lectures may also relate to unresolved tensions in Holmes's thought. For one example, Holmes seems to have looked on the aggregate of legal doctrine at any given time and place as an unstable mass characterized by internal inconsistency. Toward the end of his first lecture he generalized his views on the necessary instability and inconsistency of any given state of the law:

What has been said will explain the failure of all theories which consider the law only from its formal side, whether they attempt to deduce the *corpus* from *a priori* postulates, or fall into the humbler error of supposing the science of the law to reside in the *elegantia juris,* or logical cohesion of part with part. The truth is, that the law is always approaching, and never reaching, consistency. It is forever adopting new principles from life at one end, and it always retains old ones from history at the other, which have not yet been absorbed or sloughed off. It will become entirely consistent only when it ceases to grow.[20]

The trouble is that Holmes failed to keep in mind his own profound insight into the complex interplay between new materials drawn from life and old materials from the past which have not yet been sloughed off. He talks to us from on high, laying down principles of unrestricted universality, reducing the bases of liability to what he called, in one of the lectures on torts, a "philosophically continuous series."[21] On the face of things he purports to be making a purely descriptive statement about what the law is here and now—in Massachusetts in 1880—together with an account of how, historically, it came to be that way. But most of the time he is in fact making prescriptive statements about what the law ought to be—at all times and in all places.

The basic hypothesis in Holmes's attempt to reduce all theories of liability to a "philosophically continuous series" was one which, so far as I know, had no antecedents in the jurisprudential literature. Holmes hypothesized that the progress of the law—or of legal rules—is always toward an ideal state (which will never be reached) in which liability, both civil and criminal, will be governed by formal, external, and objective standards. In primitive legal systems, liability depends on the defendant's subjective state of mind, his intent to cause harm, or, at the least, on his having become the instrumentality through which harm is accomplished. A legal system approaches maturity to the extent that it succeeds in eliminating any reference to what the defendant actually thought, intended, or willed. In a mature system the defendant's conduct will be judged in the light of the general standards accepted in the relevant community; individual guilt or moral blameworthiness become alike irrelevant. The good man and the bad man stand equal at the bar of justice.

Holmes, wisely, never attempted to demonstrate the historical truth of his hypothesis. He seems to have thought of his hypothetical course of development— from moral, internal, subjective to amoral, external, objective—as a slow-moving glacier whose visible progress can be measured only in centuries. A startling aspect of his lectures is the repeated insistence that the principles of liability appropriate to the late nineteenth-century United States had been laid down in the English yearbooks of the fourteenth and fifteenth centuries. Most people had misunderstood what the old cases were about, principally because they had been misled by lapses into a moralistic terminology. But, with Holmes to set the record straight, it soon becomes crystal-clear that there is really no difference between a landowner in the reign of Edward IV who allowed thorns to fall onto his neighbor's land and a nineteenth-century railroad corporation whose spark-emitting engines caused damage to property adjacent to the right-of-way.

The problem to which Holmes addressed himself might be phrased thus: under what circumstances and to what extent should A be liable to B for damage or loss which B has suffered as a result of whatever it is that A has done or said or represented or promised? Holmes's answer was clear-cut: over the broadest possible range A should not be held to any liability at all; even when his liability must be conceded, the damages to be assessed against him must be kept to a minimum. These ideas, which are constantly reiterated throughout the lectures, receive their clearest expression in the course of the first lecture on torts. Holmes devoted a lengthy passage to a refutation first of Austin's view that liability was based on disobedience to the sovereign's command—thus on personal fault—and then of a view which he described as having been "adopted by some of the greatest common-law authorities" (none of whom is named) which was that "under the common law a man acts at his peril." Having disposed of his straw men Holmes continued:

> The general principle of our law is that loss from accident must lie where it falls, and this principle is not affected by the fact that a human being is the instrument of misfortune. . . .
>
> A man need not, it is true, do this or that act—the term *act* implies a choice—but he must act some-

how. Furthermore, the public generally profits by individual activity. As action cannot be avoided, and tends to the public good, there is obviously no policy in throwing the hazard of what is at once desirable and inevitable upon the actor.[22]

It is by no means clear what the link in Holmes's mind was between his hypothesis about the progress of the law toward externality and objectivity and his conclusion about the desirability of restricting or denying liability for the incidentally harmful consequences of socially useful activity. He may have hypothesized that the increasing technological complexity of civilization required an increasingly wide range of privileged activity. But the link, whatever it may have been, remained implicit; nothing in Holmes's own writing, scholarly or judicial, ever clarified the matter.

I have taken Langdell and Holmes as twin symbols of the new age, which I have called the Age of Faith. Langdell's thought was crude and simplistic. Holmes's thought was subtle, sophisticated, and, in the last analysis, highly ambiguous. Holmes's accomplishment was to make Langdellianism intellectually respectable. He provided an apparently convincing demonstration that it was possible, on a high level of intellectual discourse, to reduce all principles of liability to a single, philosophically continuous series and to construct a unitary theory which would explain all conceivable single instances and thus make it unnecessary to look with any particularity at what was actually going on in the real world. Langdellian jurisprudence and Holmesian jurisprudence were like the parallel lines which have arrived at infinity and have met.

III

In the academic world the influence of the two men was direct and immediate, consciously perceived and universally acknowledged. And the American law school, in the new format which Langdell had designed, became a principal instrument in the process of restructuring our jurisprudential thought and reshaping our legal system.[23]

The great age of the American law school has long since passed and will never come again. It may well be that no educational institutions in any country at any time have enjoyed the prestige and achieved the success of the dozen or so national law schools which grew up in the image of Langdell's Harvard. To be accepted as a student—or at all events to survive the cut at the end of the first year—at one of these schools was a guaranty of success. To be a professor of law on one of the great faculties was to hold a passport to fame and fortune.

Until Langdell's time the typical law professor had been a retired practitioner or judge—like Chancellor Kent—or a part-time instructor who devoted the bulk of his time and energy to other pursuits. Langdell recruited his faculty from recent graduates of the law school who had never practiced law and had no intention of ever doing so; they were expected to devote their full time to teaching and writing. These young men, given tenure in their twenties, sensibly responded, in an astonishing number of cases, by living into their nineties; pre-retirement tenures approaching fifty years were not uncommon. That the courses in contracts, torts, or what not were still being taught in the 1920s by professors who had joined the faculty in the 1880s gave a remarkable continuity to the educational process.

58

THE AGE OF FAITH

The law schools exerted their influence in two ways. One was the contact between professor and student in classroom, office, or law library. One of the good things about Langdell's reform was that the members of the law faculty spent—and even today continue to spend— much more of their time teaching and talking to students than the members of any other graduate faculty in any university would consider tolerable. The impact of this intense relationship between a distinguished faculty and a gifted student body seems to have been, over a long period, enormous. After your three years in Cambridge or wherever, you would never be the same again; you were stamped, branded, brainwashed for life. And the graduates of the national law schools, whether they returned to their own states or joined the new-style large law firms in New York or Boston or Philadelphia or Chicago, went on, in disproportionate numbers, to become the leaders of bar and bench in their successive generations.

The other way in which the law schools made their presence felt was through the production of a new type of legal literature. The new academic literature would have made its appearance in any case, following the success of Langdell's reform. The form which the literature took seems, however, to have been determined by an event which had nothing to do with Langdell, legal education, or jurisprudential theory. I refer to the establishment of the National Reporter System by the West Publishing Company during the 1880s.[24] Now, for the first time, all the decisions, not only of the federal appellate courts but of all the state courts of last resort, were made available to lawyers throughout the country. Being available, they had to be used: even a middle-

sized law firm in a middle-sized city could not afford to
be without a full set of reports. And, as we know to our
sorrow, the number of volumes published increased
year by year in geometric progression.

The West Publishing Company, whose interest in
jurisprudential theory I assume to have been minimal,
thus made a contribution to our legal history which, in
its importance, may have dwarfed the contributions of
Langdell, Holmes, and all the learned professors on all
the great law faculties. After ten or fifteen years of life
with the National Reporter System, the American legal
profession found itself in a situation of unprecedented
difficulty. There were simply too many cases, and each
year added its frightening harvest to the appalling glut.
A precedent-based, largely non-statutory system could
not long continue to operate under such pressures.

The new generation of Langdell-trained law professors arrived just as the situation was becoming intolerable. Fortunately, one of the basic tenets of Langdellian
jurisprudence provided the perfect remedy. That was
the proposition that "the vast majority [of cases]—
are worse than useless, for any purpose of systematic
study."[25] The earlier practitioner-oriented literature had
served to draw the reader's attention to what cases
there were. A principal function of the new academic
literature was to draw the line between the correct
cases and the vast majority of worthless ones. The
string citations of the wrongly decided cases, which
are to be disregarded, not infrequently outnumbered
the parallel strings of correct cases. The new writers
also followed the fashion, which Langdell had introduced, of using English rather than American cases
as leading authorities; the lead citation in the ritual

footnote collecting the correct cases was, almost invariably, an English case. A third feature of the new literature was its quality of bloodless abstraction. The facts of cases were rarely stated in any detail and were almost never analyzed. The customary procedure was to state the correct rule, often in black-letter text, and then proceed to justify it in terms of high-level generalities. The supporting cases came in at the bottom of the page in typically factless string citations.

It is easy to make fun of the Langdellian literature, which seems to us to have been overgeneralized and overconceptualized to a laughable degree. But we should also remember that the treatises and the law review articles represented a massive intellectual achievement. I have suggested that the new literature can be taken as a response to the pressures generated by the floods and torrents of published case reports. It is hard to see how the system could have continued to operate even tolerably well without the simplification and purification of doctrine which the system-builders proposed.

IV

We have been talking at length about the law schools and their contribution in the post–Civil War period. How should we characterize the judicial product during the same period? While the professors were constructing their reductionist theories, what were the judges doing?

The few people—including myself—who have ever spent much time studying the judicial product of the period have been appalled by what they found.[26]

The tradition of judicial creativity does seem to have survived to some degree in the federal courts. There is no point in speculating on whether the federal judges were better qualified than the state judges. If we look at the problem institutionally, it may be that the federal courts continued to benefit from the doctrine of *Swift* v. *Tyson* and the relaxed view toward precedent which that case counseled.[27] During this period the federal courts, proceeding without statutory warrant, invented the equity receivership for the reorganization of insolvent corporations—a remarkable instance of an innovative judicial response to an unprecedented economic situation.[28] Even in the federal courts, however, the pace slackens as we come down to the turn of the century. After 1900 the Supreme Court withdrew from the decision of private law questions and became a forum for the resolution of political controversies dressed up as issues of constitutional law. Without the Supreme Court to superintend, coordinate, and synthesize, the federalizing—or nationalizing—principle of *Swift* v. *Tyson* became a headless monster, marked down for destruction by all right-thinking men.[29]

As the federal courts went out of the business of making new law, the state courts, of necessity, took their place. In the earlier period the state courts had been quite as innovative as the federal courts. Gibson of Pennsylvania, Shaw of Massachusetts, Kent in New York—and many others—were judges of preeminent stature who made law with all the enthusiasm of a Marshall or a Story.[30] But when, after the Civil War, the state courts came into their inheritance, the supply of great judges seemed, almost overnight, to vanish. Except for Holmes in Massachusetts, it is hard, even for someone who is familiar with the literature, to summon up the name of a single judge.

The judicial product of the period can fairly be de-

scribed as Langdellianism in action. I do not mean to
suggest that, at least in the beginning, the judges were
consciously following or adopting or copying Dean
Langdell's theories. The truth must have been the other
way around. Langdell had intuitively sensed that the
Civil War marked a watershed in our legal history, as it
did in our political history, that a new age had dawned,
that a new approach to law had already come into
being. Langdell had nothing to do with creating the
new age or with shaping the new approach. He was,
however, the first to give a conscious, theoretical expression to the new order of things—which is why he
became the symbol of his time.

The post–Civil War judicial product seems to start
from the assumption that the law is a closed, logical
system. Judges do not make law: they merely declare
the law which, in some Platonic sense, already exists.
The judicial function has nothing to do with the adaptation of rules of law to changing conditions; it is restricted to the discovery of what the true rules of law
are and indeed always have been. Past error can be
exposed and in that way minor corrections can be
made, but the truth, once arrived at, is immutable and
eternal. Change can only be legislative and even legislative change will be treated with a wary and hostile
distrust. A statute in derogation of the common law—
as what statute is not?[31]—will be strictly construed even
if it cannot be set aside on constitutional grounds as
beyond the power of the legislature to enact.

This predisposition of the judges reflected itself in
the style of opinion-writing which came into vogue.
This became the age of the string citation—quite as
much in the judicial opinions as in the learned treatises.

And the judges, like the professors, rarely, if ever, bothered with the facts of the cases they cited or with the reasons why the cases had been decided as they had been. Nor did the judges make any attempt to explain the reasons for their decisions. It was enough to say: The rule which we apply has long been settled in this state (citing cases). Indeed, it was improper, unfitting, unjudicial to say more. The juice of life had been squeezed out; the case reports became so many dry husks. Stare decisis reigned supreme.[32]

The judges who thought this way and wrote this way set their faces against change. During this period the courts became the apostles of reaction and the guardians of a romanticized, oversimplified past. It is highly appropriate that the problems of labor organization and of industrial accidents long continued to be dealt with as parts of the law of master and servant—a turn of phrase which helped greatly to soften and blur the grim reality of life in, say, a steel mill in Pittsburgh or Gary. The legislatures, stirred by populist discontents, experimented with social legislation—regulating the hours and conditions of employment, restricting the exploitation of women and children, and so on. The courts routinely struck down these statutes on one or another ground—the most amusing ground having been the great principle of freedom of contract. That is to say, if a ten year old child wants to work twelve hours a day in a textile mill, by what warrant is the legislature empowered to deprive the child's parents of their right to enter into such a contract on his behalf? This attitude toward social legislation entrenched itself in the Supreme Court of the United States where, over the dissents of Holmes and Brandeis, it continued to command a

majority long after the state courts had abandoned
their root-and-branch opposition to anything new.[33]

V

Why should all of this—indeed, why should any of this
—have happened?

It may be that every legal system, at some point in its
development, goes through its Age of Faith. Sooner or
later a Blackstone or a Langdell appears. The idea of a
body of law, fixed for all time and invested with an
almost supernatural authority, is irresistibly attractive
—not only for lawyers and their clients but, perhaps
even more, for the populace at large. If a Blackstone or
a Langdell comes at the right time, he will be heard and
his words will, for a generation, be devoutly believed:
his message is a comforting one and ought to be true
even if it is not.

Since Langdell was heard and was believed, he
evidently came at the right time. The fact that it took
the English seven hundred years to produce their Blackstone while we produced our Langdell in seventy years
merely serves to underline the accelerating tempo of life
from the eleventh century to the nineteenth. By Langdell's time we had put behind us the problems which had
concerned Kent and Story: how the common law of
England should be adapted to the conditions of life in
the United States, how a reasonable degree of national
uniformity in the substantive law could be achieved in
a decentralized federal republic.[34] We had accumulated a
respectable number of our own precedents and, in
addition, we had the English reports to draw on. The
building materials were there; all we needed was someone to tell us how to go about putting them together.

The circumstances of life in the post–Civil War United States contributed to the success of Langdell's mission. After the terrible convulsion of the war we were in need of peace, repose, and tranquility: our energies as a nation were spent. Our politics degenerated into a sort of mush with two indistinguishable parties offering indistinguishable candidates to choose between. Our anarchists and militants were so far outside the mainstream of popular thought that only the unhappy victims of their assassination attempts had anything to fear from them.

The pace of technological progress slowed during this period. Anyone born in 1800 who lived until 1860 experienced the shock of technological change. Anyone born in 1850 who lived until 1910 experienced relatively little change except for the addition, toward the end of the period, of a few amenities like central heating and indoor plumbing. The great inventions which have unsettled our own lives did not have their impact until much later. Rapid technological change unsettles the law quite as much as it unsettles people. The slow pace of change during the half century after the Civil War contributed to the illusion that a stable body of law was not only a theoretical possibility but an accomplished fact.

The post–Civil War period saw the emergence of large-scale business enterprises, along with the vast fortunes which they generated. Undreamed-of aggregates of capital presented unheard-of problems for solution. The traditional bias of liberal theory in favor of the least possible governmental intervention—that government is best which governs least—made a sort of nonsense when you had to factor the railroads, the

Standard Oil Trust, and United States Steel into the
equation. On the other hand, laissez-faire economics
had an obvious appeal to the movers and shapers of
our economy. The theoretical structure which would
leave the masters of the new wealth free to do their
own thing in their own way was promptly provided.
There has always been a symbiotic relationship between
the academic establishment, which provides the theories,
and the economic establishment, which appreciates
being told that the relentless pursuit of private gain is
the best way of serving the public interest.

In recent years it has become a truism to point out
that laissez-faire economics and late nineteenth-century
legal theories are blood brothers.[35] The hostility which
the courts showed toward social legislation was a
merely superficial manifestation of this relationship.
On a deeper level the legal theorists who preached the
doctrines of limited liability—the loss must lie where it
falls—and of the lowest possible damages shared a
community of interest with their economic counter-
parts who preached the religion of laissez-faire. And
the quality of abstraction which came to characterize
most legal writing seems like the mirror image of the
idealized models of the economists. Even the economists
must have felt a grudging admiration for the lawyers
who could see that the case of a workingman bargaining
with his corporate employer over wages and the case
of a Vermont farmer dickering with a summer resident
over the price of a cord of firewood could both be
reduced to the paradigm of A who voluntarily contracts
with B.

I have credited Holmes with the original formulation
of most of these theories—although I should add that

Holmes never shared the prevalent hostility toward social legislation. Holmes had no great sympathy for such legislation—he thought that most of it was silly and useless—but he consistently maintained his position that the dominant political majority is entitled to work its will on its defeated adversaries.[36] The other ideas all seem to have come from Holmes. Like Langdell before him, Holmes had intuitively sensed the felt necessities of the time and had succeeded in giving a magisterial expression to apparently revolutionary ideas which had, unnoticed, already worked their way into the common law. The stalwarts of the post-Holmesian orthodoxy took from the master only what suited them; the disturbing and heretical aspects of his thought were ignored.

4

The Age of Anxiety

I

All Ages of Faith may well be of brief duration. The pleasant and comforting myth of the law's internal consistency and external stability cannot, for long, sustain itself. The facts of life cannot, for long, be suppressed. Every Blackstone must have his Bentham; every Langdell must have his Llewellyn. The specifics of the breakdown, like the specifics of the original construction, are determined by the accidents of time and place.

From the vantage point of the 1970s it is clear enough that the great structure of Langdellian jurisprudence crumbled during the period between the two World Wars. It did not, of course, come tumbling down all at once like the walls of Jericho at Joshua's trumpet-blast. And the truth of the matter may be that the spirit of Langdellianism survived the apparent rout of the Langdellian forces during the bitter jurisprudential battles of the 1920s and 1930s—just as the spirit of Rome may be said to have survived the collapse of empire to reappear in the guise of the Catholic church.[1] But even if, for the sake of the argument, we concede the identity of the two Romes, we may go on to observe that the style and trappings of Catholic Rome were quite different from the style and trappings of Imperial Rome.

We can be equally sure that a revivified and resurgent
Langdellianism would bear little outward resemblance
to the original.[2]

The most extraordinary aspect of our Age of Faith
seems to me to have been the universality of a shared
belief, the absence of dissent, the politeness of debate
with an opposition whose proudest boast was its loyalty,
the power of the reigning establishment to charm its
natural opponents into conformity. Thus Louis Dembitz
Brandeis, a Jewish lawyer from Kentucky with populist
sympathies, could have a sensationally successful career
at the Boston bar.[3] Thus Roscoe Pound, a reformed
botanist from Nebraska who had advocated what was
then called sociological jurisprudence, could become
dean of the Harvard Law School.[4] Thus the progressives,
who in a later generation would style themselves liberals,
could outdo the conservatives in their fervent attachment to the American dream.[5] Reform, in those happy
days, meant building up, not tearing down.

After 1900 the Langdellians themselves became reformers. The American codification movement had
apparently died about the time of the Civil War; nothing
had been heard from or about it since then.[6] In the
1890s the American Bar Association set up an affiliate
or subsidiary which it called the National Conference
of Commissioners on Uniform State Laws. The Conference went to work on a series of statutes designed to
codify various aspects of commercial law, which had
always been the preferred area of operation of the
proponents of codification. Within a twenty-year period
half a dozen statutes, of which the most important were
the Negotiable Instruments Law and the Uniform Sales
Act, had been drafted, promulgated, and widely en-

acted.[7] The presence of the American Bar Association as an approving sponsor makes clear that the codifying statutes were not the work of wild-eyed revolutionaries. But why should codification suddenly have become respectable?

Langdellian jurisprudence had been an attempt to achieve unity of doctrine on the case-law level.[8] Langdell and his followers were common lawyers to a man. The "one true rule of law" idea had been almost immediately subjected to intolerable pressures by the mounting flood of case reports. The writers of the great treatises sought to keep the situation under control by carefully distinguishing between the relatively few correct cases (many of them English) and the great piles of trash which filled the bound volumes of the reports. However another aspect of our late nineteenth-century theory caused trouble at exactly this point. Judges were not supposed to make law; they merely followed precedents. So, what was a judge who took the stare decisis business seriously—as many did—supposed to do when it turned out that the precedents in his state were, according to the learned gentlemen from Cambridge, wrong? The disunity of American case law from state to state may indeed have increased during the latter part of the nineteenth century as the nationalizing principle of *Swift* v. *Tyson* lost its strength. The *Swift* v. *Tyson* device had not infrequently succeeded in producing nationally acceptable solutions to regionally controverted issues.[9] As that device passed out of use, American case law apparently faced a bleak future of rampant parochialism.

American interest in codification had been stimulated by then recent English developments. The English, on their home turf, had paid not the slightest attention to

Jeremy Bentham's strident manifestos calling for universal codification. The Benthamite idea was more attractive when the question became how best to secure the benefits of English civilization—including English law —for India. At all events, the English undertook and patiently carried out the ambitious project of providing India with English-inspired codes. The success of the Indian project led to a hesitant beginning in codifying some of the more troublesome areas of domestic law with the Bills of Exchange Act (1882) and the Sale of Goods Act (1893). Having gone so far, the English stopped and proceeded no further. Their two Victorian codifying statutes are still in effect. Proposals for further codification in this century have, after a flurry of initial publicity, been quietly abandoned.[10]

The American codifiers seem to have assumed that their function was to free judges, crippled by their devotion to stare decisis, from the fetters of aberrant precedents in unenlightened jurisdictions. Indeed, the only truly enlightened jurisdiction was what was referred to in moot court competitions at the Harvard Law School as the State of Ames.[11] But with the law of Ames made available to all in statutory form, the true light could shine everywhere.

Statutes like the Uniform Sales Act were not statutes at all. That is, they were not designed to provide rules for decision. Drafted in terms of loose and vague generality, they were designed to provide access to the prevailing academic wisdom. The rules for decision in sales cases were to be found, not in the Uniform Sales Act which had been drafted by Samuel Williston of the Harvard Law School, but in Professor Williston's treatise on the law of sales.[12] This aspect of the codifica-

tion was, apparently, generally understood. The courts
—and counsel—paid no attention at all to the Sales
Act; they paid enormous attention to Professor Williston's treatise. What we had was not so much a codification as a non-codification—a method of preserving the
common law purged of all impurities.

The idea that the early twentieth-century codifiers
were interested in common law preservation rather than
statutory reform smacks of paradox. The idea, however,
becomes less paradoxical in the light of the next major
law reform project, which was undertaken in the 1920s
and which enlisted the support of the groups which had
earlier supported the uniform statutes. The American
Law Institute, whose membership included the most
distinguished lawyers, judges, and law professors of the
time, was founded for the purpose of preparing a series
of authoritative statements—which for some reason
were called Restatements—of the principal branches
of the common law: contracts, torts, agency, trusts,
property, and so on.[13]

The Restatements, although cast in statutory form,
were not designed to be (and were not) enacted as
statutes by any legislature. The idea or the hope was
that the Restatement formulations would exert a persuasive, even a compelling, force in purging the common
law of eccentricities which might have arisen in particular jurisdictions and in promoting a soundly based
uniformity throughout the country. The Restatements
can be taken as a more direct method of achieving the
same results which, earlier in the century, had been
pursued through codification of the commercial law.
Samuel Williston, who, following the success of the
Sales Act, had become the quasi-official draftsman for

the National Conference of Commissioners on Uniform States Laws, became the Chief Reporter for the American Law Institute's *Restatement of Contracts.*

There were a great many unresolved ambiguities about the Restatement project. Were the Restaters supposed to be "codifying" the law as it was? In situations where conflicting rules had evolved, were they supposed always to choose the "majority rule" over the "minority rule"? If a common law rule was felt to be unsatisfactory or unjust, were they at liberty to "restate" a "better rule" as determined by the membership of the Institute? If the law appeared, at the time of drafting, to be changing—with an old rule being abandoned and a different rule in course of being formulated—what were they supposed to do about that? The official position of the Institute on such issues was purely Langdellian: there were such things as the fundamental principles of the common law, which did not change; those principles, or most of them, were known, having been set out in the treatises which had proliferated for fifty years past; those principles (and not idiosyncratic cases) were the subject matter of the Restatements. No doubt most of the people who were caught up in the Restatement project shared the Institute's official position.

Blackstone's *Commentaries,* which advocated the preservation of English law without change, were written at a time when English law was undergoing violent, rapid, and fundamental change.[14] We can now see that, from the 1920s on, American law was entering into a period of comparable change. The Restatements, like the *Commentaries,* may be taken as the reaction of a conservative establishment, eager to preserve a threatened status quo. Like the *Commentaries,* the Restatements were applauded by most right-thinking men and may, for a time, have served their purpose.

The *Digest of Justinian* had collected, for the use of sixth-century Byzantium, the wisdom of third-century Roman jurisprudence. Not since the *Digest* had there been anything quite like the American Restatements. The fate of both these extraordinary legal artifacts was the same: the hurricane continued to howl; the foundations continued to slip away; the wisdom of the past could not save.[15]

We may take the provision in successive generations of the commercial law codifying statutes (which were not really statutes) and of the Restatements (which were merely a better expression of the same idea) as having obscurely reflected a realization on the part of the Langdellians—who enthusiastically supported both ventures—that things were not going as they were supposed to go, as for a generation or more they had appeared to be going.

II

Our dawning Age of Anxiety is perfectly symbolized by the mysterious—the almost mystical—figure of Benjamin Nathan Cardozo.[16] Cardozo's father had been a corrupt lower court judge allied with the Tweed Ring in New York, who had suffered disgrace when Tweed's organization was broken up. The son apparently felt that his mission was to redeem his father's sins. Ascetic in his personal tastes, he decided at an early age to renounce the pleasures and temptations of the world in favor of a life of intellectual meditation. The accounts of all those who knew him tell us of a man of compelling personal charm as well as of great sweetness of character. By the unanimous testimony of his contemporaries, Cardozo was a saint.[17]

Before his appointment to the Supreme Court of the United States in succession to Holmes, Cardozo served for nearly twenty years on the New York Court of Appeals and evidently dominated that great court, intellectually, throughout his tenure. Cardozo was a truly innovative judge of a type which had long since gone out of fashion. In his opinions, however, he was accustomed to hide his light under a bushel. The more innovative the decision to which he had persuaded his brethren on the court, the more his opinion strained to prove that no novelty—not the slightest departure from prior law—was involved. Since Cardozo was one of the best case lawyers who ever lived, the proof was invariably marshalled with a masterly elegance. It is not until the reader gets to the occasional angry dissent that he realizes that Cardozo had been turning the law of New York upside down.[18] During his twenty years Cardozo succeeded to an extraordinary degree in freeing up—and, of course, unsettling—the law of New York. It is true that he went about doing this in such an elliptical, convoluted, at times incomprehensible, fashion that the less gifted lower court New York judges were frequently at a loss to understand what they were being told.[19]

In 1920 Cardozo delivered a series of Storrs Lectures at the Yale Law School. Holmes's *The Common Law* and Cardozo's *The Nature of the Judicial Process* (the title under which his Yale lectures were published) are the two most celebrated books in the history of American jurisprudence.[20] The two books, however, have nothing in common beyond the facts that nobody reads them and everybody praises them.

Cardozo's book, as a matter of strict fact, has almost no intellectual content. He addressed himself to the problem of how a judge goes about deciding a case. In the great majority of all cases, he said, the outcome is foredoomed; the past has foreclosed the present. Only in an occasional case does the process of adjudication involve a creative act on the part of the judge. In such a case, Cardozo suggested, the judge may—indeed must— look to what he called the "methods" of philosophy, history, tradition, and sociology. By the "method of sociology"he meant that the judge, at least in a situation where he finds nothing else to guide him, is to take into account the effect of his decision on social or economic conditions.[21] Toward the end of his last lecture he introduced what might be called the theme of judicial anguish:

> I was much troubled in spirit, in my first years on the bench, to find how trackless was the ocean on which I had embarked. I sought for certainty. I was oppressed and disheartened when I found that the quest for it was futile. I was trying to reach land, the solid land of fixed and settled rules, the paradise of a justice that would declare itself by tokens plainer and more commanding than its pale and glimmering reflections in my own vacillating mind and conscience. . . . As the years have gone by, and as I have reflected more and more upon the nature of the judicial process, I have become reconciled to the uncertainty, because I have grown to see it

as inevitable. I have grown to see that the process in its highest reaches is not discovery, but creation; and that the doubts and misgivings, the hopes and fears, are part of the travail of mind, the pangs of death and the pangs of birth, in which principles that have served their day expire, and new principles are born.[22]

The thing that is hardest to understand about *The Nature of the Judicial Process* is the furor which its publication caused. Nothing can better illustrate the extraordinary hold which the Langdellian concept of law had acquired, not only on the legal but on the popular mind. Cardozo's hesitant confession that judges were, on rare occasions, more than simple automata, that they made law instead of merely declaring it, was widely regarded as a legal version of hardcore pornography. By this unseemly indiscretion, it was suggested, Cardozo had forfeited any claim he might otherwise have had to be considered as a fit candidate for a seat on the Supreme Court of the United States. In time the furor abated and he took his seat on the Supreme Court without any visible sign of public indignation. But a less saintly man than Cardozo might, in 1920, have found himself running close to the reefs of impeachment.[23]

Cardozo was, we might say, a revolutionary *malgré lui* who was affectionately attached to the structure which, imperceptibly, almost surreptitiously, he proceeded to subvert and destroy. There was however, nothing affectionate, imperceptible, or surreptitious about the procedures of the group, based mostly in the law schools, who came to be known as the Legal

Realists. They appeared to be in favor of tearing everything down. On further analysis the case may prove to be
that, just as Cardozo was a revolutionary *malgré lui,* the
Realists were Langdellians *malgré eux.* In times of revolutionary change, it is hard to tell who is on which side.

What the curious episode which we call American
Legal Realism was about has long been a puzzle not
only to outsiders but to the participants. Karl Llewellyn,
whom most people regarded as the leading Realist,
insisted throughout his life that there had never been a
Realist "school" or a Realist "movement." Professor
William Twining, one of the few English scholars who
has studied our transatlantic law-ways, seems to have
concluded, in a recent book on Llewellyn and the
Realist Movement, that Legal Realism, if there was
such a thing, was an exclusively American phenomenon
which bore no relationship to any developments, past
or present, in any other legal system.[24] Indeed Professor
Twining suggests, by implication, that Legal Realism
was, so to say, a play-off for the Ivy League champion-
ship, with the combined faculties of the Columbia and
Yale Law Schools taking the field against Harvard.
There was more to it than that.

In a narrow sense, the Realist controversy consisted
of a series of articles which appeared in the law reviews
during the 1930s and which, today, makes up as dreary
a course of reading as anyone can hope to find anywhere.[25] When Llewellyn denied that there had ever
been a Realist school or movement, he was, presumably,
referring to the law review controversy. On the law
review level, the issues at stake, which had never been
clearly defined, became progressively more confused

and more insubstantial as the debate went on. But neither Llewellyn nor anyone else ever denied that a fundamental shift in American legal thought had taken place in the decades following World War I.[26]

The one thing on which the academic theorists who emerged after World War I agreed was that the traditional or Langdellian way of achieving doctrinal unity on the level of case law or Restatement was absurd. However, in demonstrating the absurdity, the new generation of theorists used as their principal weapon one which Langdell himself had provided: the idea that the reported cases are the laboratory materials for our systematic or scientific study.[27] In its Langdellian version that had meant that we were to study a few correct cases and disregard the rest. The post-Langdellians proposed to look at all the cases.

Arthur Corbin may have been the first, as he was the greatest, of the post-Langdellian scholars.[28] Corbin took no part in the Realist controversy; in any event, his intellectual formation had been complete long before World War I. Llewellyn, who had studied under Corbin and had been closely associated with him, regarded Corbin as his spiritual father in the law. Indeed, all the Realists treated Corbin with a respect which they showed to almost no other figure of his generation.

Corbin counseled not only that we should study all the cases but that we should study them not so much for their doctrinal statements as for what he liked to call their "operative facts." Furthermore, Corbin practiced what he preached, not only in his teaching but in his writings which culminated in his great treatise on contracts. In Corbin we no longer find the high-level generalities supported by factless string citations which had characterized the Langdellian literature, whose greatest achievement had been the other great treatise on contracts written by Corbin's dear friend and life-long opponent, Samuel Williston.[29] In Corbin we find painstaking factual analyses of all the cases, even those of minor importance which are relegated to the foot-notes. Indeed the practice of paying an obsessive regard to the facts of cases, while disregarding their doctrinal content, became after World War I, and has since remained, a characteristic of most American legal scholarship.

Unity of doctrine cannot survive that way of dealing with cases. The process of disintegration is already evident in Corbin's own work. In Anglo-American law it has, for several centuries, been customary to say that contractual liability will not be imposed on a promisor unless his promise is supported by something called consideration. Corbin concluded that there is not, and never has been, such a thing as a, or the, doctrine of consideration. At various times and in various places and in a great variety of circumstances, courts have imposed contractual liability. The only purpose of studying the field is to determine under what circum-stances the liability has been imposed. There is no harm, Corbin cheerfully concluded, in using the word *con-sideration* which has been bequeathed to us by history. But, he added, if you want to use it, you should be aware that it means, and always has . meant, many different and inconsistent things.[30]

Some of those who followed in Corbin's footsteps carried his teaching to the point of intellectual nihilism. Wesley Sturges, whom generations of students at the

Yale Law School revered as the greatest of teachers, was one.[31] Early in his career Sturges published a few law review articles which were of an almost unbelievably narrow scope and focus—for example, an elaborate study of the North Carolina case law on the nature of mortgages, a subject of no conceivable interest to Sturges or anyone else.[32] The point of the study was to demonstrate that the North Carolina law of mortgages made no sense and could most charitably be described as a species of collective insanity on the march. At about the same time he put together a casebook for a new course which he called Credit Transactions: the casebook consisted principally of the most absurd cases, along with the most idiotic law review comments, which he had been able to find.[33] The law, as Wesley Sturges conceived it, bore a striking resemblance to the more despairing novels of Franz Kafka. Sturges himself had the courage of his bleak convictions. *Ex nihilo nihil.* He wrote almost nothing during the remainder of his long career.[34] No one could match Sturges in his penetrating analysis of the most complex legal materials, but he saw no point in playing children's games. I was his student and served on his faculty while he was dean of the Yale Law School: he was a lonely, great, and tragic figure.

III

The process of disintegration of unitary theory and of return toward a pre-Langdellian pluralism, already apparent in Corbin's work, became even more marked in the work of Corbin's disciple, Karl Llewellyn.[35] In 1930 Llewellyn published a casebook on sales, which broke with tradition by including a great deal of analyt-

ical and historical material as well as by supplementing
the leading cases reprinted in full with digests of hundreds, if not thousands, of related cases. He followed the
casebook with a series of magisterial articles on sales
law.[36] In both the articles and the casebook he traced,
in meticulous detail, the development of sales law in
the United States from the 1800s to his own time.
Llewellyn's work in sales, like Corbin's work in contracts, was designed to prove that the apparent unity of
the orthodox version of sales law (represented by Williston's treatise on sales and by the Uniform Sales Act
which Williston had drafted) had been achieved by a
serious distortion of historical fact and truth. Llewellyn,
however, went well beyond Corbin in articulating his
own theoretical position. The essential vice in the
Willistonian construct, as Llewellyn saw it, was the
attempt to derive all the rules of sales law from a few
general principles, assumed to be universally applicable.
The remedy lay in what Llewellyn referred to as "narrow
issue thinking." Under Williston's Sales Act, for example, the remedies available on breach depended on
whether seller or buyer owned ("had the property in")
the goods at the time of the breach. The rules for determining when the property passed from seller to buyer
became complicated, even metaphysical, but the thresh-
old question in Sales Act litigation had to be the
resolution of the property issue. Llewellyn's thesis was
that the entire property concept should be scrapped
along with the idea that all contracts of sale should be
treated alike. Transactions between professionals (or
merchants) should be treated differently from transactions in which a professional sold goods to a non-
professional (or consumer). Sales for resale should be

treated differently from sales for use. Distinctions should be made between sales for cash and sales on credit; present sales and future sales; one-shot or single delivery transactions and long-term contract arrangements. Llewellyn's atomization of sales law, like Corbin's atomization of contract law, was at the opposite pole from the Langdellian attempt to reduce all principles of liability to what Holmes had called a "philosophically continuous series."[37]

Llewellyn's chosen field was one which had already been codified. For that reason his articles were for the most part attacks on the Uniform Sales Act coupled with proposals that the Sales Act should be replaced with a statute which would reflect (as the Sales Act did not) the actual practices of businessmen in the twentieth century. It is rarely a reformer's lot to have the opportunity to carry out the reforms which he has advocated. Llewellyn did indeed become the principal draftsman of what was initially known as the Uniform Revised Sales Act and later became the Uniform Commercial Code. The Code (which is now in force in all American jurisdictions except Louisiana) was the most ambitious project of law reform which has been carried out in this century. What came out of the labors of Llewellyn and many others over the better part of twenty years is the best example that can be found of the confusions and crosscurrents of American law during the protracted period of the Code's drafting.[38]

The Code was jointly sponsored by the National Conference of Commissioners on Uniform State Laws (which had acquired a de facto monopoly of commercial law codification)[39] and the American Law Institute (which had completed the Restatement project[40] but

was, like any organization, reluctant to shut up shop
and go out of business). The Conference had access to
the state legislatures; the Institute had access to money;
at the relevant time William Schnader, a Philadelphia
lawyer, held high office in both organizations and is
credited with having arranged their unlikely collaboration. While the memberships overlapped to some extent,
the Conference was predominantly made up of small-
town lawyers; the typical Institute member was a
senior partner in a prestigious law firm or a federal
judge or a law school dean. Most Commissioners and
most members of the Institute were conservatives—not
only in politics but in jurisprudence.

There is a comforting irony in the fact that the Conference and Institute not only chose Karl Llewellyn as
principal draftsman (or Chief Reporter) for the Code
but succeeded in living with him for fifteen years on
terms of mutual respect and amity. Llewellyn in the
1930s had become the symbol of the academic revolt
against Langdellianism and orthodoxy. He was flam-
boyant both in his personality and his prose style. He
must have seemed, to most members of both Conference
and Institute, unsound. On the other hand, Llewellyn
had been a devoted member of the Conference for
many years and had become the Conference's principal
draftsman in commercial law matters.[41] He was also,
beyond question, the preeminent academic authority
on sales law (which was the starting point for the Code
project): a revised Sales Act without Llewellyn's par-
ticipation would have been as unthinkable as a *Restatement of Contracts* without Williston's. In all probability, Llewellyn thought that he could persuade his
employers to adopt his own theories. In turn, the people
who controlled the Conference and Institute thought

that they could make use of Llewellyn's drafting skills
and encyclopedic knowledge of the law, while reserving
the power to veto any excesses toward which their
unpredictable Chief Reporter might seek to lead them.

On the whole and in the long run the conservatives or
traditionalists had their way. Llewellyn's proposals for
a radical restructuring of the law—as, for example, in
distinguishing between the standards applicable to
"merchants" and those applicable to non-merchants—
survived the early drafts only in an attenuated, watered
down, almost meaningless form. Provisions which
would have notably increased the liability of manufacturers for their defective goods were simply deleted
from the later drafts. Not only the substance but the
style of the Code changed dramatically as the drafting
process continued. Llewellyn himself had had the concept of what he called a "case law code"—by which he
meant a statute whose principal function would be to
abrogate obsolete rules, thus leaving the courts free to
improvise new rules to fit changing conditions and
novel business practices. Llewellyn's code, as he conceived it, would have abolished the past without attempting to control the future. That jurisprudential
approach did not satisfy the groups of practicing lawyers
who participated in the project and whose influence
increased as the drafting approached the final stages.
These lawyers had perhaps become uneasily aware of
mounting indications of a new style of judicial activism.[42]
At all events they insisted on a tightly drawn statute,
designed to control the courts and compel decision.
To a considerable degree, they got what they wanted.

The Code in its final form can best be described as a
compromise solution which satisfied no one. Llewellyn
had recruited a drafting staff which was composed

mostly of younger law professors whose own ideas about law had been greatly influenced by Llewellyn and the other Realists. Sharing Llewellyn's views, they produced drafts which reflected his own pluralism and anti-conceptualism. Those drafts were largely rewritten by practitioners whose instinctive approach to law was more conventional. Even so, the Code, as rewritten, retained more than mere traces of the earlier approach, both in substance and in style. It testifies to the fundamental cleavage which, by the 1940s, had overtaken the legal profession in this country.

It was the curious fate of the Code, a 1940s statute, not to have been widely enacted until the 1960s. In the 1950s the legal establishment which controlled the bar associations (and had great influence with the bankers' associations) opposed the Code and was successful in preventing its enactment. In the 1960s the same people who had fought the Code ten years earlier had reversed their field and were counted among its most vigorous supporters. A plausible reason for this reversal is that during the 1950s the courts, in a surge of activism, had themselves been rewriting much of the law. The Code, which in the 1940s had seemed much too "liberal" to its conservative critics, had by the 1960s become an almost nostalgic throwback to an earlier period. The final irony in the Code project was that its eventual "success" (that is, its enactment) can well be taken as an attempt by the most conservative elements in the bar to turn the clock back.

IV

At least in the law schools, the jurisprudential revolution had, by 1940 or thereabouts, won a complete success.[43] (And it should be borne in mind that what is taught in the law schools in one generation will be widely believed by the bar in the following generation.) The "conceptualism" of the Langdellian period was, by everyone except a few die-hard traditionalists, held up to scorn. The great treatises and the Restatements which had followed in their wake were pilloried as nonsensical attempts to portray the life of the law as having been logic rather than experience: it was assumed that the treatises would not (and should not) have any successors. The idea that the process of judicial decision was much more irrational than it was rational had a fashionable currency. With the solitary exception of Holmes, the theorists and system-builders of our vanished Age of Faith were caricatured as simpleminded reactionaries.

And yet the revolution may have been merely a palace revolution, not much more than a changing of the guard. My own thought has come to be that the adepts of the new jurisprudence—Legal Realists or whatever they should be called—no more proposed to abandon the basic tenets of Langdellian jurisprudence than the Protestant reformers of the fifteenth and sixteenth centuries proposed to abandon the basic tenets of Christian theology.[44] These were the ideas that "law is a science" and that there is such a thing as "the one true rule of law."

At the hands of the Realists, the slogan "law is a science" became "law is a social science." Where Langdell had talked of chemistry, physics, zoology, and botany as disciplines allied to the law,[45] the Realists talked of economics and sociology not merely as allied disciplines but as disciplines which were in some sense part and parcel of the law. Economists, sociologists, and even psychiatrists were invited to join the faculties of the major law schools and did so in considerable numbers. What were called non-legal materials began to appear in the casebooks, which themselves became "Cases and Materials" to indicate that studying law no longer meant studying the cases which, according to Langdell, were our "experimental materials."

Few lawyers ever bothered to study any of the social sciences (any more than the social scientists, even those who joined the law faculties, ever bothered to study law). But from the 1930s on, it became an article of faith for a great many lawyers and law professors that the social sciences had come much closer to the "truth" than traditional legal scholarship had ever done. The social scientists agreed with this flattering estimate of their work.

The work of such scholars as Corbin had popularized the idea that what counted in the law was not abstract doctrine but concrete facts. The fact-sensitivity to which American lawyers had been conditioned was, I suggest, one of the factors which accounted for their enthusiastic acceptance of the social science idea. The facts underlying a transaction or a business practice or a social custom can be glimpsed in judicial opinions only as through a glass darkly. The courts themselves, burdened by procedural limitations and restricted to adversary proceedings, are poor institutions for finding out what the essential facts are or were. The individual judge is a nonspecialist with respect to the economic or social background of the cases which come before him and is not supposed to go beyond the record made by counsel. Thus the inadequacy of judicial fact-finding techniques makes judicial opinions worthless as accounts of what is actually going on in the world.

It appeared, however, that the social scientists, particularly the sociologists, had made great advances in techniques of empirical research. If the law professors adopted those techniques, they could marshal the facts on which enlightened decision depends. Since the 1930s a great many empirical study projects on legal issues have been undertaken, typically funded by lavish foundation grants and publicized at well-attended press conferences. The fate of most of these projects has been to wither on the vine without producing any fruit. It is a fact of life that thinking or talking about doing empirical research is much more fun than actually doing it. And even if you have the resources to employ armies of research assistants to gather all the facts there are, the gathered facts have a disappointing way of turning out not to mean anything beyond themselves. However, despite the skeptical opinion which has just been expressed, research projects which can be described as "empirical" have been, and continue to be, popular both with university administrations and with foundations (which do have to find some way of spending their money).

The lawyers who became fact-gatherers and thought of themselves as social scientists had to provide themselves with sets of values or goals. These could be, and usually were, drawn from whichever of the "allied disciplines" an individual lawyer was familiar with: Keynesian (or anti-Keynesian or pseudo-Keynesian) economic theory, stimulus-response or Freudian psychology, current theories in vogue among anthropologists or sociologists, and so on. Myres McDougal (whose training had been in law) and Harold Lasswell (who had started his career as a political scientist) collaborated on the elaboration of a system of juris-

prudence which they called policy science.[46] The central
feature of the McDougal-Lasswell system was a set of
basic values (such as wealth, power, rectitude, enlightenment, and so on) which were defined in terms of high-
level generality. Developments in the law were to be
analyzed and evaluated in the light of the basic values
on which, it was assumed, all reasonable men would
agree. Despite the novelty of its trappings, the work of
McDougal and Lasswell, particularly in its insistence
that everything can be reduced to a few general principles, can, not unfairly, be taken as a return toward
older theories of law and as a reaction against the
pluralism of such scholars as Corbin and Llewellyn.

A great deal of the legal writing which was published
through the 1940s took on a political coloration which,
before World War I, had been called progressive, then,
somewhat later, liberal, and was finally associated with
the New Deal of the 1930s. There were no doubt many
reasons for the leftward-leaning political allegiance of
the post-Langdellians, which in many individual instances may not have been a matter of deeply held
conviction. In any case, the emerging patterns of post-
World War I liberalism, which was destined to hold
political power for a generation, were perfectly tailored
to fit the preconceptions of Realist jurisprudence.

The Realists, who were deeply concerned with social
and economic problems, had little use for the judicial
process. The obvious alternative to a judicial solution of
such problems is a legislative solution. A legislative
committee, unlike a court, can analyze a problem in
depth and cut through to a rational solution. If continuing supervision or regulation is required, an administrative agency which will quickly develop its own

expertise is the answer. In the first flush of enthusiasm, doing all this seems like child's play. Jeremy Bentham seems to have believed that running up a comprehensive code for England, France, or the United States would be as easy as rolling off a log. In this country in the twentieth century we have had more than our fair share of Jeremy Benthams.

The idea of governmental intervention to improve the quality of life became the stock-in-trade of the progressive movement.[47] States which came under the influence of progressive ideology—Wisconsin under the LaFollettes, Pennsylvania under Gifford Pinchot—were hailed as laboratories for experiments in social progress. The possibility that the experiments might fail seems never to have been seriously considered. With the coming of the New Deal the opportunity for experimentation on a much grander scale was at hand. Many of the academic Realists, gladly forsaking their lives of scholarly research, enlisted for the duration and were among the leading movers and shakers of the New Deal period. They drafted statutes by the gross and set up administrative agencies by the score. Having created a new world, they rested and hallowed it. But the problems did not go away, and Utopia was as remote as ever. What to do about these mouldering statutes and elderly agencies will presently become an urgent problem of law reform.

V

While the legal scholars were becoming social scientists and the legal activists were drafting statutes and administering agencies, what were the judges doing? The conventional wisdom of the 1930s was that judicial power was a relic of the dead past. The Realists had stripped the judges of their trappings of black-robed infallibility and revealed them to be human beings whose decisions were motivated much more by irrational prejudice than by rules of law. The law, state and federal, was in process of being reduced to statutory form with most of the significant continuing problems being committed to administrative agencies. The judicial role was bound to become progressively more modest, more mechanical, more trivial. What happened, as is frequently the case, was the opposite of what the conventional wisdom assumed.

The activism of the Warren Court in areas of public or constitutional law has for a long time been a matter of public praise or blame. The truth is that the birth, or rebirth, of judicial activism considerably antedated the formation of the Warren Court and has been quite as much a factor to be reckoned with in the state courts as in the federal courts and in areas of private law as in areas of public law.[48] Present prospects are that this surge of activism will continue, no matter who may sit on the Supreme Court of the United States or on our less august tribunals.[49]

In an earlier chapter, I suggested that the post–Civil War judges and theorists seemed, on the obscure level of instinct, to be working toward the same goals.[50] The patterns which the theorists provided and the results which the judges arrived at were in perfect harmony. Characteristic of our post–Civil War jurisprudence was its fondness for abstraction and for building unitary theories as well as its insistence on restricting both liability and damages.

No doubt the obscure correspondence between theory

and practice holds true in any period. It has surely been true in this century that the reforms which the professors called for in their law review articles were already being provided, or had been provided, by the judges, without anybody having noticed what had happened. The universal abstractions faded, the unitary theories disappeared, the range of liability became wider and wider and plaintiff's damages flourished like the green bay tree.[51]

The rebirth of judicial activism has gone hand in hand with a rebirth of the federalizing or nationalizing principle. In 1938 the Supreme Court declared that the federal law doctrine of *Swift* v. *Tyson* was, and always had been, unconstitutional.[52] The *Swift* v. *Tyson* device, which had over a long period been of great service, had ceased to work in this century. The only sensible course was to get rid of it, as the Supreme Court did. But, having scrapped the machine that no longer worked, the Court immediately set about providing a substitute that would work.

Even at the time the *Erie* case was decided, a prescient observer might have commented that the case's apparent meaning could hardly be taken as its true meaning. Control over the development of the substantive law was not going to be returned to the states at a time when the powers and presence of the federal government had reached a point unknown in our history. And that proposition, which was clearly enough true in the years preceding World War II, had long since passed the point of no return by the time we had come to the end of the war period.

The post-*Erie* federalization of the law was not established by the fiat of a single great case.[53] The federalizing principle has expressed itself in a variety of ways as the courts have reacted to the reality of ever-increasing federal power. Insofar as a principle has emerged, it is that the presence of any kind of federal interest in a case is enough to support the conclusion that decision should be governed by federal law rather than by the law of any state. Thus, contracts to which the United States, in any of its manifold capacities, is a party are contracts governed by federal law. The presence of a federal regulatory agency may lead to the conclusion that all the transactions in which the members of the regulated industry engage are governed by a uniform federal law to be supplied by the courts. It was once assumed as a matter of course that gaps in an incomplete federal statute were to be filled in in the light of principles borrowed from the common law—that is, the law of some state. That approach has been superseded by the idea that federal statutes generate a common law penumbra of their own: gaps are to be filled in by a process of extrapolation from whatever the court conceives the basic policy of the statute to be. Under the federal Constitution many areas of the law—admiralty, bankruptcy, and patents are obvious examples—are, in some sense, federal specialties. Nevertheless, until about the time of World War II the federal courts in deciding such cases routinely applied rules of state law in any situation where it did not appear that a specialized federal rule already existed. Since World War II the Supreme Court of the United States has given a wide currency to the ideas that, in federal specialty areas, a federal rule must be "fashioned" if one does not already exist and that a proper regard for federal supremacy requires the application of the federal rule even if the

forum of litigation is a state court.[54] This aspect of the
New Federalism goes well beyond the federal law
doctrine of *Swift* v. *Tyson*. Under that doctrine federal
courts were not bound by rules of state law, but state
courts were under no duty to follow a federal rule.[55]
Under the emerging federal supremacy doctrine, state
courts will be bound by rules of federal law over an
area which will itself grow as the powers of the federal
government grow.

During the period when the apparent meaning of the
Erie case was taken to be its true meaning, federal
judges suffered much frustration when the state law
rule by which, under *Erie*, they were bound turned out
to be one which the state supreme court had announced
fifty or seventy-five or a hundred years earlier and never
since then reconsidered. The increasing localization of
many types of litigation in the federal courts aggravated
the problem. However, with the emergence of the
federal rule-fashioning technique, no federal judge who
has the slightest flair for his craft need any longer be
concerned with even the most horrifying clinker which
he may pick up from the nineteenth-century dustheap.

Between 1900 and 1950 the greater part of the substantive law, which before 1900 had been left to the
judges for decision in the light of common law principles,
was recast in statutory form. We are just beginning to
face up to the consequences of this orgy of statute
making. One of the facts of legislative life, at least in
this country in this century, is that getting a statute
enacted in the first place is much easier than getting
the statute revised so that it will make sense in the light
of changed conditions. On the federal level it is difficult
to the point of impossibility to draw the attention of a

crisis-ridden Congress to any area of law reform which, although it may be urgent, has not erupted in political controversy. And the more tightly a statute was drafted originally, the more difficult it becomes to adjust the statute to changing conditions without legislative revision.[56] Unfortunately, with the New Deal, a style of drafting which aimed at an unearthly and superhuman precision came into vogue, on the state as well as the federal level.

Eventually the problem of obsolescent statutes solves itself. No statutory draftsman has a crystal ball in which he can read the future. The best he can do is to make some kind of sense out of the recent past. A well-drafted statute will deal sensibly with the issues which have come into litigation during the twenty or twenty-five years which preceded the drafting. However, the focus of litigation has a way of shifting unexpectedly and unpredictably. New issues, which no one ever dreamed of, present themselves for decision. With luck, the statute will turn out to have nothing to say that is relevant to the new issues, which can then be decided on their own merits. In this way any statute gradually becomes irrelevant and will finally be reabsorbed within the mainstream of the common law. But that takes a long time.[57]

The most difficult period in the life of a statute—as in the life of a human being—is middle age. Admittedly the statute is no longer what it once was but there is is life in the old dog yet. An occasional subsection still has its teeth and subparagraph (3)(b) may burn with a gem-like flame. We are now passing through our statutory middle age.

Statutory language—like any other kind of language

—almost always presents alternative possibilities of construction. There will, however, be cases in which even the most disingenuous construction will not save the day. In such a case, it has always been assumed, a court must bow to the legislative command, however absurd, however unjust, however wicked. Once the legislature has taken over a field, only the legislature can effect any further change.

So far as my own knowledge takes me, it is only within the past ten or fifteen years that there have been suggestions in some judicial opinions to the effect that courts, faced with an obsolete statute and a history of legislative inaction, may take matters into their own hands and do whatever justice and good sense may seem to require. These suggestions have, for the most part, been put forward with an understandable degree of hesitant reluctance. As the idea becomes more familiar to us, I dare say that we will come to see that the reformulation of an obsolete statutory provision is quite as legitimately within judicial competence as the reformulation of an obsolete common law rule. Indeed, if we do not, we will presently find ourselves lost in a legal jungle with no hope of finding a way out.[58]

The New Federalism has largely freed us from the problem of obsolete judicial decisions on the state level. Obsolete decisions handed down long ago by the Supreme Court of the United States are coming to be a serious problem of obviously difficult solution. The Court, which is quite as crisis-ridden as Congress, is able to decide only a small fraction of the cases which are submitted to it. The energies of the Justices are taken up with grave issues of public order. Even if they had the time, they no longer have the expertise to deal with the issues of private law which, fifty or seventy-five years ago, accounted for a significant part of the Court's work. Since the Supreme Court will not, indeed cannot, reconsider many of its own arguably obsolete holdings, the time may have come for the inferior federal courts to experiment with the idea that, in case of need, they should not follow or consider themselves bound by obsolete Supreme Court cases—which would be a much cleaner approach to the problem than refined and artificial distinctions which lead only to states of intolerable complexity. In all probability, the worst fate that such innovative federal judges would have to fear would be reversal; it is unlikely that they would be impeached.[59]

5

On Looking Backward and Forward
at the Same Time

I

For two hundred years we have been in thrall to the eighteenth-century hypothesis that there are, in social behavior and in societal development, patterns which recur in the same way that they appear to recur in the physical universe.[1] If the hypothesis is sound, it must follow that, once the relevant developmental sequences which have led us to our present state have been correctly analyzed, we will know not only where we are but where we are going. Our understanding of the present will enable us to predict the future and, within limits, to control it. Once the forces at work are known, they can be channeled or harnessed to serve the needs and wants not necessarily of mankind at large but at least of those who are in a position to manipulate them.

We have never had to face up to that frightening possibility for the excellent reason that no historian, social scientist, or legal theorist has ever succeeded in predicting anything. After two hundred years of anguished labor, the great hypothesis has produced nothing. The formulations proposed in each generation have collapsed when the realities of the following generation have become known. Nevertheless, the dream dies hard. Each new generation of investigators has convinced itself that the cause of past failure lay in inadequate methodology and that, with more refined techniques, the trick will finally be pulled off. The historians continue to ransack the archives. The sociologists continue to perfect increasingly complicated ways of carrying on their empirical studies. It is true that some economists, having observed the fate of all the theories put forward by their predecessors, have succumbed to skepticism and seem ready to go out of the long-term prediction business.

One lesson which we can draw from all this is that the hypothesis is itself in error. Man's fate will forever elude the attempts of his intellect to understand it. The accidental variables which hedge us about effectively screen the future from our view. The quest for the laws which will explain the riddle of human behavior leads us not toward truth but toward the illusion of certainty, which is our curse. So far as we have been able to learn, there are no recurrent patterns in the course of human events; it is not possible to make scientific statements about history, sociology, economics—or law.

The assumption that we are engaged in an endeavor that can be properly described as scientific has clouded the vision and distorted the thinking of generations of legal scholars. The Legal Realists of the 1930s embraced the fallacy quite as enthusiastically as the Langdellian formalists.[2] As a group, the Realists unquestioningly accepted the idea of the "one true rule of law" which was waiting to be discovered if only the search was conducted in the right way. Realist jurisprudence proposed a change of course, not a change of goal.

The idea that "law is a science" has conditioned all our responses. It has dictated to us both what we were looking for and how we were to go about looking for it. If we can rid ourselves of the illusion that law is some kind of science—natural, social, or pseudo—and of the twin illusion that the purpose of law study is prediction, we shall be better off than we have been for at least a hundred years.

II

We took from the eighteenth century not only its belief in science but also its belief in the inevitability of progress. The two ideas are, indeed, closely linked. Science and progress go hand in hand. If we believe in science, we accept progress as its natural consequence. If we lose faith in the scientific method (at least as applied to social phenomena), we will also turn away from the belief in the perfectability of our society.

In the grisly aftermath of World War II the genial optimism which had for so long sustained us seems to have become, to many minds, no longer tenable or even tolerable. The dominant mood of our own bleak time may well have become a pervasive doubt or malaise, which easily modulates into a black despair at the human condition and its prospects..

One of the ways in which our twentieth-century despair has manifested itself has been in our changing attitudes toward the past. So long as we believe in ourselves, we look to the past (if we look to it at all) for instructive moral lessons designed to illustrate how and why everything necessarily works out for the best. When we cease to believe in ourselves, we look urgently to the past, not for instructive moral lessons, but in the desperate attempt to find out what went wrong. If only we could find that out, we instinctively feel, we could reverse our mistaken course and take whatever corrective measures might be necessary. Or, on a more reasoned level, we may feel that some understanding of our past mistakes may help us cope with our obscure present and unknown future. It is surely true that each generation gets the past it deserves. The fall of Rome and the collapse of empire set off reverberations in the late twentieth-century mind which were undreamed of a hundred or even fifty years ago.

During periods of apparent social dissolution the traditionalists, the true believers, the defenders of the status quo, turn to the past with an interest quite as obsessive as that of the radicals, the reformers, and the revolutionaries. What the true believers look for, and find, is proof that, once upon a time, things were as we should like them to be: the laws of economics worked; the streams of legal doctrine ran sweet and pure; order, tranquillity, and harmony governed our society.[3] Their message is: turn back and all will be well.

Until 1960 or thereabouts, American legal literature was ahistorical or even antihistorical. The treatises and the law review articles which date from our Age of Faith dealt with the historical development of the field of law under consideration with perfunctory disinterest. The writers devoted their considerable talents to the exposition of the present state of the law— which, by implicit and universal assumption, was also the final state, change having, by 1900, been abolished.

After World War I, when it became obvious that the reports of the death of change had been exaggerated, the legal profession became obsessed with the need to keep up with the times. The annual pocket-part, which collects all the latest cases and statutory changes, became a standard feature of most treatises and practitioners' manuals. In the 1930s loose-leaf services were invented which kept their subscribers up-to-the-minute with monthly or weekly releases. Since the 1950s the computerization of all legal materials, with instant access to everything, has opened up nightmarish possibilities.[4]

In the law schools, until some time after World War II, the study of any field of law from a historical point of view was almost unheard of. Indeed, the Realists (with the exception of Karl Llewellyn) were no more interested in the past than the Langdellian formalists had been.[5] In the history of legal thought in this country few events are more interesting, or can have been more surprising to contemporary observers, than the explosion of interest in what has come to be called legal history.[6] Beginning in the late 1950s courses and seminars billed as "historical" appear, for the first time, in the law school catalogues. What is more, these offerings have been, and continue to be, largely subscribed by interested students. During the same twenty-year period the law reviews have published more historical material, written for the most part by the younger generation of academic lawyers, than had, I dare say, been published over the preceding hundred years. Indeed, specialized journals devoted exclusively to the publication of articles on legal history have made their appearance, and the academics who look on themselves as legal historians have organized in groups, sections, and associations. Since the foundations follow the fashions, there is even a good deal of money in the legal history game— an idea which, a generation ago, would have seemed fanciful.

I assume that the hold which legal history has currently acquired on the legal imagination is one reflection of the crisis of Western thought. In the writing of legal history, as in the writing of general history, both left-wing revisionists and right-wing traditionalists have been active. No doubt, the past is here to stay, but what the past really was becomes, each year, a little more obscure. The one thing that is clear is that no one, except speakers on ceremonial occasions, any longer believes the comforting eighteenth-century myth about the inevitability of progress.

III

The extraordinary achievement of our first half century of law may well have contributed to the excesses of the following half century. In the 1870s it must have been tempting to conclude that since, through law, much had been achieved, it followed that, through law, everything could be achieved, including the ultimate goals of scientific prediction and the control of the future course of our society. In the 1970s we look back on an unpleasant half century which has been largely devoted to destroying the illusions which had commended themselves to the men of the 1870s.

It is not surprising that, during this unpleasant period, the official legal establishment, in one of the great advertising campaigns of all time, sought to sell the integrity of the legal product, warranted to insure the salvation of our society. The idea of law was ridiculously oversold, which led to great confusion in the public mind when it became clear that ours is a government not of laws but of men and that justice under law is notably unequal.

May 1 of each year has been set aside as Law Day. On that day, speakers go forth from the bar associations to expound to the Rotary Clubs and the high schools the virtues of the Rule of Law in a Free Society. What is meant by the Rule of Law is rarely explained with any particularity, but the message is clear: we have the Rule of Law; our enemies do not have the Rule of Law; our possession of the Rule of Law is what makes our society a better society than their society.

The Rule of Law idea has also had its advocates on a less absurdly politicized level. In its respectable academic version the idea emphasizes principally the importance of procedural due process, the nice observance of established rules, the right of the accused to confront his accuser in open court before he is sent to jail.[7] Academics who promote the Rule of Law have also been, almost without exception, enthusiastic promoters of one or both of two ideas which enjoyed a great vogue during the 1950s. One was the idea which was summed up in the slogan: the End of Ideology. That meant that, in the United States as of 1950 or thereabouts, all the great social, political, and economic issues had been, for all time, satisfactorily solved. All that remained was to keep the great machine running smoothly—a maintenance job for technicians. The other idea also had its slogan: World Peace through

World Law—an attractive proposition which enlisted
the suffrage of many men of good will. World Peace
through World Law seemed to mean that all disputes
between nations not only should but could be settled
by courts (or international organizations like courts)
in the light of legal rules drawn up ahead of time.
Implicit in the World Peace through World Law idea
was the assumption that the territorial division and
the distribution of power in the world, as it existed
in the 1950s, was on the whole satisfactory and should
not be changed.

The three slogans—the Rule of Law, the End of
Ideology, World Peace through World Law—all assumed that the society we had achieved in the 1950s
was a good one, that it must be preserved from attack
by its enemies (who were usually identified as the
Communist powers or, more broadly, the adherents
of Marxist ideology), and that the function of law was
to insure stability and guarantee us against change.
The leading spokesmen for these ideas in the 1950s
thought of themselves, and were thought of by others,
as liberals in the great tradition. They were supporters
of the New Deal reforms and many of them had held
office under Roosevelt and Truman, as they later did
under Kennedy and Johnson. The greatest difficulty
in understanding what was going on in the United
States through the 1950s is that ideological positions
which now seem to have been conservative or reac-
tionary were then seriously put forward as liberal,
even radical.

The cheerfully meaningless slogans of the 1950s have
not survived the national and international chaos of
the 1960s and 1970s. The End of Ideology and World

Peace through World Law already have a quaintly old-fashioned sound, and it is only an occasional unreconstructed cold warrior who still proclaims the virtues of the Rule of Law. But the conservative reaction which inspired the political slogans may, on a much more sophisticated level, still be with us.[8]

In 1970 I delivered a series of lectures which were later published under the catchy but misleading title, *The Death of Contract.* I ended the last of the lectures in this way:

> We have witnessed the dismantling of the formal system of the classical theorists. We have gone through our romantic agony—an experience peculiarly unsettling to people intellectually trained and conditioned as lawyers are. It may be that, in this centennial year, some new Langdell is already waiting in the wings to summon us back to the paths of righteousness, discipline, order, and well-articulated theory. Contract is dead— but who knows what unlikely resurrection the Easter-tide may bring?[9]

In 1970 I thought of the passage I have quoted as merely a rhetorical flourish which, I hoped, might induce the audience to leave quietly without actually throwing things at me. I seem to have been a better prophet than I had dreamed of being. Our new Langdell may not yet have made his appearance on front-and-center stage but it is already apparent that the cause of well-articulated theory has been better served in the 1970s than, arguably, it has been in any decade since the 1870s. Forsaking the pluralism of such scholars as Corbin, Llewellyn, and Kessler,[10] the New Conceptualists, as they have been dubbed in some quarters, have returned to the elaboration of unitary theories, to the reduction of all principles of liability to Holmes's "philosophically continuous series."[11] Their work is being taken seriously, as of course it should be. In the world of legal scholarship the New Conceptualism will be a force to be reckoned with for at least the next generation. It is, however, unlikely that its future includes a triumph as complete as that of Langdellianism a century ago. In the polarized society which we seem to have arrived at, consensus is an unlikely issue.

The vice of the formalistic approach to law, on the level of serious scholarship as on the level of political slogans and advertising campaigns, is that it leads to a disastrous overstatement of the necessary limits of law. In our own history, both in the late nineteenth century and in our own time, the components of the formalistic approach have included the search for theoretical formulas assumed to be of universal validity and the insistence that all particular instances should be analyzed and dealt with in the light of the overall theoretical structure. Solutions to problems are "right" if they conform to, "wrong" if they deviate from, that structure. The theoretical model itself quickly becomes frozen, so that what was "right" or "wrong" in 1870 must be equally "right" or "wrong" in 1920; what is "right" or "wrong" in 1970 will be equally so in the no doubt magical year of double twenty. The adept of formalism, once he has perfected his model (or borrowed one ready-made from an economist or a sociologist), becomes an advocate of stability and an enemy of further change. This process takes place quite as inexorably with respect to theories or models which were in their origins radical or revolutionary as it does with respect to those which in their origins were conservative or traditionalist. Thus during periods when the formalistic approach is dominant, the stare decisis idea inevitably comes to the fore along with the idea that the courts, without legislative sanction, are precluded from making any innovations on their own. Decision becomes a mechanistic process in which it is forbidden to look beyond the letter of the statute and the holding of the last case. The result, both in the legal mind and in the popular mind, is the deeply held belief that law is an engine for curbing our social ills through an enforced adherence to predetermined patterns of behavior.

I do not propose that we embrace chaos and all become anarchists as the only escape from the excesses of formalism. I do suggest that the lesson of the past two hundred years is that we will do well to be on our guard against all-purpose theoretical solutions to our problems. As lawyers we will do well to be on our guard against any suggestion that, through law, our society can be reformed, purified, or saved. The function of law, in a society like our own, is altogether more modest and less apocalyptic. It is to provide a mechanism for the settlement of disputes in the light of broadly conceived principles on whose soundness, it must be assumed, there is a general consensus among us. If the assumption is wrong, if there is no consensus, then we are headed for war, civil strife, and revolution, and the orderly administration of justice will become an irrelevant, nostalgic whimsy until the social fabric has been stitched together again and a new consensus has emerged. But, so long as the consensus exists, the mechanism which the law provides is designed to insure that our institutions adjust to change, which is inevitable, in a continuing process which will be orderly, gradual, and, to the extent that such a thing is possible in human affairs, rational. The function of the lawyer is to preserve a skeptical relativism in a society hellbent for absolutes. When we become too sure of our premises, we necessarily fail in what we are supposed to be doing.

When we think of our own or of any other legal system, the beginning of wisdom lies in the recognition that the body of the law, at any time or place, is an unstable mass in precarious equilibrium. The study of our legal past is helpful to lawyers and judges and legislators in the same way that the study of recorded games is helpful to a chess player. But the principal lesson to be drawn from our study is that the part of wisdom is to keep our theories open-ended, our assumptions tentative, our reactions flexible. We must act, we must decide, we must go this way or that. Like the blind men dealing with the elephant, we must erect hypotheses on the basis of inadequate evidence. That does no harm—at all events it is the human condition from which we will not escape—so long as we do not delude ourselves into thinking that we have finally seen our elephant whole.

IV

I shall conclude by paraphrasing Holmes.[12]

Law reflects but in no sense determines the moral worth of a society. The values of a reasonably just society will reflect themselves in a reasonably just law.

The better the society, the less law there will be. In Heaven there will be no law, and the lion will lie down with the lamb. The values of an unjust society will reflect themselves in an unjust law. The worse the society, the more law there will be. In Hell there will be nothing but law, and due process will be meticulously observed.

Notes

PREFACE

1. The concluding lecture in the series was published, substantially in the form in which it was delivered (with the addition of a few footnotes), in the *Yale Law Journal* under the title "The Age of Anxiety" (84 *Yale L. J.* 1022 (1975)). The material covered in that lecture now appears as Chapters 4 and 5.

CHAPTER 1

1. S.F.C. Milsom, *Historical Foundations of the Common Law* xi (1969).

2. The entries under the heading "jurisprudence" in the *New Oxford Dictionary* suggest that the first uses of the word to mean "philosophy of law" date from the nineteenth century. In earlier English usage the word had referred to legal systems generally or to their study.

3. There will, perhaps, be general agreement that economics and sociology were eighteenth-century inventions. My suggestion that history was another may seem, at first blush, surprising, since historical writing in the Western intellectual tradition goes back at least to the Greeks and Romans. What I have in mind, as the following discussion in the text indicates, is that, with Hegel and other writers, a radically different approach to the study of history manifested itself which emphasized not only a highly professionalized use of the source materials but a quest for the underlying "laws" of historical development. For a fascinating study of these changing attitudes, see M. Mandelbaum, *History, Man and Reason—a Study in Nineteenth-Century Thought* (1971). C. Becker, *The Heavenly City of the Eighteenth-Century Philosophers* (1932) is still one of the most illuminating discussions of eighteenth-century thought.

4. William Blackstone (1723–1780) was the first holder of the Vinerian professorship of law at Oxford, to which he was appointed in 1758. His *Commentaries on the Laws of England* was first pub-

lished between 1765 and 1769. It has been estimated that a thousand copies of the English edition were sold in this country (at £10 the set) before the first American edition (at £3 the set) was published in 1771–1772. Many other editions of the *Commentaries* appeared throughout the nineteenth century. See Lockmiller, *Sir William Blackstone*, 170–171 (1938). D. Boorstin, *The Mysterious Science of the Law* (1941) is an excellent study of Blackstone's ideas, which are for the most part incomprehensible to the twentieth-century mind.

5. William Murray, First Earl of Mansfield (1705–1793), was born in Scotland but made his career in England. He was educated at Oxford and was called to the bar in 1730. He held a number of political posts before becoming Chief Justice of the Court of King's Bench in 1756; he served in that capacity until 1788. His opinions are notable for their salty wit, their almost complete irreverence for the past, and their extraordinary sensitivity to the actual practices of the mercantile community. Mansfield established a "jury" of London merchants and was accustomed to seek their advice on mercantile custom and practice in commercial cases.

6. The case was Pillans and Rose v. Van Mierop and Hopkins, 3 Burr. 1663, 97 Eng. Rep. 1035 (K.B. 1765). A London banking house had agreed in writing to honor a draft to be drawn on it by a Rotterdam banking house for the account of an Irish client of the London house. Before the Rotterdam draft was presented, the Irish merchant had failed; the London bankers refused to pay. Held: the promise to honor the draft was binding; judgment for the Rotterdam bankers. Mansfield's use of the case as a vehicle to abolish the consideration doctrine is of particular interest in the light of the fact that the other justices on the court, who wrote concurring opinions, had no difficulty in finding, on one theory or another, a "consideration" for the defendant's promise to honor the draft. The "strange and absurd" comment quoted in the text is from the concurring opinion of Justice Wilmot. Mansfield's colleagues on the court usually merely noted that they agreed with Lord Mansfield. The fact that they delivered elaborate concurring opinions in Pillans and Rose may suggest that they felt that, on this occasion, the Chief Justice had gone too far.

7. For the rejection of Mansfieldianism in England, see 8 W. Holdsworth, *A History of English Law* 34 *et seq.* (2d ed. 1937); 12 *id.* 595 *et seq.* (1938).

8. L. M. Friedman, *A History of American Law* (1973) contains,

in Part I, a lively account of American law during the colonial
period. Professor Friedman's interesting book, the bulk of which is
devoted to the nineteenth-century story, appears to be the first
attempt at a comprehensive survey of the development of American
law.

9. See Friedman, note 8 *supra*, 282–285. A volume of Connecticut
reports was published in 1789; a volume of Pennsylvania reports
appeared the following year. Dallas, the editor of the Pennsylvania
volume, became the first Reporter of the cases of the Supreme Court
of the United States.

10. The practice of having only one opinion for the majority of
a multi-judge court seems to have been instituted by Marshall when
he became Chief Justice of the Supreme Court of the United States.
Marshall's practice came under attack and, as late as the 1820s,
proposals were made under which each of the Justices who sat on a
case would have been required to file a separate opinion. See Roe
and Osgood, United States Supreme Court: February Term 1824,
84 *Yale L. J.* 770, 772 (1975), citing C. Haines, *The Role of the
Supreme Court in American Government and Politics* 512 *et seq.*
(1944). The attacks failed and "the opinion of the court" became the
standard practice in all American courts, state and federal. Indeed
in some Western states, dissenting judges were not infrequently
assigned to write the official opinion for the majority—an apparently
nonsensical practice which actually makes a good deal of sense. If
the court is divided, it is the part of wisdom to make the opinion as
narrow as possible, which a judge who disagrees with the majority
can be counted on to do.

11. K. N. Llewellyn, *The Common Law Tradition: Deciding
Appeals* (1960). Karl Nickerson Llewellyn (1893–1962) was one of
the most interesting and original figures in twentieth-century American jurisprudence. A graduate of the Yale Law School, he practiced
law briefly in New York City in the early 1920s and, from then until
his death, served on the faculties of the Columbia and the University
of Chicago Law Schools. In Chapter 4 *infra* I shall have a good deal
to say about Llewellyn's work. On Llewellyn and his time, see W.
Twining, *Karl Llewellyn and the Realist Movement* (1973), which I
reviewed in 22 *Am. J. of Comparative Law* 812 (1974). I attempted to
gave my own appreciation of Llewellyn in an obituary notice which
appeared in 71 *Yale L.J.* 813 (1962).

Llewellyn's book, *The Common Law Tradition*, was the outgrowth

of a series of Storrs lectures which he delivered at the Yale Law
School in 1940. The original lectures were never published.

12. See, e.g., Horwitz, "Historical Foundations of Modern Con-
tract Law," 87 *Harv. L. Rev.* 917 (1974); D. Kennedy, *The Rise and
Fall of Classical Legal Thought (1850–1940)* (a forthcoming book by
Professor Kennedy, who has graciously given permission to cite it).
L. Friedman, note 8 *supra*, also seems to accept Llewellyn's periodi-
zation.

13. The post–World War I developments are discussed in Chapter 4 *infra*.

14. "I recognize without hesitation that judges do and must legislate but they can do so only interstitially; they are confined from
molar to molecular motions. A common-law judge could not say I
think the doctrine of consideration a bit of historical nonsense and
shall not enforce it in my court." Southern Pacific Co. v. Jensen,
244 U.S. 205, 231 (1917) (dissenting opinion). On whether a
"common-law judge" could abolish the doctrine of consideration,
see Lord Mansfield's decision in Pillans and Rose v. Van Mierop
and Hopkins (K. B. 1765), discussed *supra*, note 6 and accompanying text. Of course, a great deal of water had gone over the dam
between Lord Mansfield's day and Justice Holmes's day.

15. "The life of the law has not been logic; it has been experience.
The felt necessities of the time, the prevalent moral and political
theories, intuitions of public policy, avowed or unconscious, even
the prejudices which judges share with their fellow-men, have had a
good deal more to do than the syllogism in determining the rules by
which men should be governed." *The Common Law* 5 (Howe ed.
1963)—a book which will be extensively discussed in Chapter 3
infra.

CHAPTER 2

1. See generally L. Friedman, *A History of American Law* 93 *et
seq.*, 265 *et seq.* (1973). On the first American law schools, see R.
Stevens, "Two Cheers for 1870: The American Law School," in
Law in American History 405, 407 *et seq.* (eds. D. Fleming and B.
Bailyn, 1971). The date "1870" in Professor Stevens's title refers to
the reorganization of the Harvard Law School under Dean Langdell
—an event which will be discussed in Chapter 3 *infra*.

2. On attitudes toward the civil law during the post-Revolutionary

period, see Stein, "The Attraction of the Civil Law in Post-Revolutionary America," 52 *Va. L. Rev.* 403 (1966).

3. See W. W. Crosskey, *Politics and the Constitution in the History of the United States* (1953). Most constitutional law experts of the time, in a series of savage reviews, condemned Professor Crosskey to the ninth circle of hell. My own thought (speaking as a non-expert) is that Crosskey was in error on a great many peripheral details but may well have been right on his central argument. See my discussion of the attacks on Crosskey in "The Age of Antiquarius: On Legal History in a Time of Troubles," 39 *U. of Chi. L. Rev.* 475, 485 *et seq.* (1972). Crosskey's thought was that the intent of the framers had been subverted in the course of the growing controversy about slavery and that in particular James Madison had later falsified his notes on the Constitutional Convention (which were not published until 1840, after Madison's death). The two volumes which Crosskey published in 1953 were designed as an introduction to a series of volumes. Because of ill health he was unable to continue the work. Thus the proof of Madison's falsifications (if indeed there was any proof) was never produced.

4. In Wheaton and Donaldson v. Peters and Grigg, 33 U.S. (8 Pet.) 591, 658 (1834) McLean, J., wrote for the Court: "It is clear, there can be no common law of the United States. The federal government is composed of twenty-four sovereign and independent states; each of which may have its local usages, customs and common law. There is no principle which pervades the union and has the authority of law, that is not embodied in the constitution or laws of the union. The common law could be made a part of our federal system only by legislative adoption.

"When therefore a common law right is asserted, we must look to the state in which the controversy originated."

The case was an action by Wheaton, who had been the Reporter of the Supreme Court's opinions from 1816 to 1827, against Peters, his successor in that office. Peters, on becoming Reporter, had issued an abbreviated edition of his predecessor's volumes (which had contained a great deal of commentary in addition to the opinions themselves). Peters's edition of the opinions for the Wheaton years sold for much less than Wheaton's Reports and effectually destroyed their market. Wheaton claimed that Peters had infringed his copyright. Judgment was for Peters. G. Dunne, *Justice Joseph Story and the Rise of the Supreme Court* (1970) has an interesting discussion of the case (at p. 323 *et seq.*).

5. Frontier attitudes toward law and lawyers are brilliantly examined in P. Miller, *The Life of the Mind in America (from the Revolution to the Civil War)* (1965). On lay judges and the situation in New York, see Friedman, note 1 *supra*, 109 *et seq.*, 122 *et seq.* W. E. Nelson, *Americanization of the Common Law: The Impact of Legal Change on Massachusetts Society, 1760–1830* (1975), is a remarkable study of many of the matters discussed in this section.

6. See Friedman, note 1 *supra*, 97. The word "English" does not appear in the statute as quoted by Professor Friedman but seems to be required by the overall sense.

7. On Lord Mansfield see Chapter 1, note 5 *supra* and the accompanying text. On the rejection in England of Mansfield's innovations after his death, see Chapter 1, note 7 *supra*.

8. See note 11 *infra* and the accompanying text.

9. I discussed the early codification movement in a paper delivered to a Conference on Comparative Commercial Law at McGill University in September 1968. See "Commercial Law in the United States: its Codification and Other Misadventures" in *Aspects of Comparative Commercial Law* (eds. J. Ziegel and W. Foster) 449 (1969).

10. Jeremy Bentham (1748–1831) savagely attacked Blackstone's idealized version of the common law in his *Fragment on Government*, first published anonymously in 1776. In his strenuous advocacy he seems to have idealized the virtues of a codified law quite as much as Blackstone idealized those of the common law. Bentham has become known as the father of utilitarianism, although many of his ideas have come to us as filtered through the Victorian minds of James and John Stuart Mill. J. Rawls's *A Theory of Justice* (1971) is a critical examination of the utilitarian premise which has provoked much controversy among philosophers and jurisprudentially inclined lawyers. At his death Bentham left a vast mass of manuscript which has never been (and may never be) published. One of Bentham's major works was first published in 1945 under the title *The Limits of Jurisprudence Defined*. Professor H. L. A. Hart of Oxford and his collaborators have been working on a new edition of Bentham which has resulted in the publication of *An Introduction to the Principles of Morals and Legislation* (eds. J. Burns and H. L. A. Hart 1970) and

Of Laws in General (ed. H. L. A. Hart 1970). See also H. L. A. Hart, "Bentham and the Demystification of The Law," 36 *Mod. L. Rev.* 2 (1973). One of Professor Hart's theses is that the Mills, thought to be Bentham's disciples, had in fact distorted and diluted many of Bentham's ideas. A recent study of Bentham is C. Atkinson, *Jeremy Bentham: His Life and Work* (1969).

11. The name of Joseph Story (1779–1845) will frequently recur in the following discussion. The best account of Story's career is G. Dunne, *Justice Joseph Story and the Rise of the Supreme Court* (1970), which I reviewed in 39 *U. of Chi. L. Rev.* 244 (1971). Appointed to the Supreme Court by President Madison in 1812, he served until his death. Beginning in 1831 he also served as Dane Professor of Law at Harvard and, in that capacity, produced a series of remarkable treatises (which will presently be discussed). His advocacy of a state-level codification as a means of avoiding the dangers referred to in the text was contained in an address on "The Progress of Jurisprudence" delivered to the Suffolk Bar Association, September 4, 1821, published in *The Miscellaneous Writings of Joseph Story* 198, 237 (1852). The *Miscellaneous Writings* were edited by Story's son, William Wetmore Story.

12. The reference in the text is to Story's 1837 "Report on the Codification of the Common Law," submitted to the Governor of Massachusetts on behalf of a commission which had been appointed to consider a codification of the law of the Commonwealth. The Massachusetts codification project was abandoned after Story declared that he would be unable to serve as draftsman of the projected code. His report for the commission is published in *The Miscellaneous Writings of Joseph Story* 698 (1852). The "mischievous . . . or futile" line appears at p. 712; the passage on "commercial contracts," which includes a list of the types of contracts he had in mind, is at pp. 730–731.

13. David Dudley Field (1805–1894) devoted himself throughout his long career to the cause of codification both nationally and internationally. In 1847 he was appointed to a commission charged with preparing a Code of Civil Procedure for New York. That Code, enacted in 1848, was thereafter substantially rewritten on several occasions. (See Friedman, *A History of American Law* 340 *et seq.* (1973).) In the 1850s Field became the guiding spirit of a commission charged with codifying the entire corpus of New York law, sub-

stantive as well as procedural. The five Codes, which were produced in an incredibly short period, were enacted by the New York legislature in 1878, but vetoed by the governor. That was the end of the New York codification movement but the Field Codes were adopted in the Dakota Territories in 1865 (the then governor was a close friend of Field) and in California (somewhat revised to meet local conditions) in 1872. (David Field's younger brother Stephen, who later became a Justice of the Supreme Court of the United States, seems to have been responsible for the enactment of his brother's Codes in California, to which he had emigrated following the Gold Rush.) The California Codes were subsequently enacted in several other Western states. The California courts shortly adopted the principle that the Codes should be construed as having adopted the rules of the common law (whatever those rules might be or become); thus the provisions of the Codes appear to have had little or no effect on the development of California law. (On the subsequent history of the Field Codes in California, see Harrison, "The First Half-Century of the California Civil Code," 10 *Calif. L. Rev.* 185 (1922)). Opinions on the merits of Field's Codes have varied. Sir Frederick Pollock (who had been a draftsman himself) apparently despised them. See the *Holmes-Pollock Letters* (ed. M. Howe, 2d ed. 1961), Pollock's letters of July 18, 1918 ("the New York abortion") and May 11, 1927 (referring to the Western states which had "foolishly adopted" the Field Codes). What has most interested me in my own (fragmentary) study of the Codes (principally the Civil Code provisions on Contracts) has been the extent to which Field introduced civil law principles in what was supposed to be a common law codification. On Field see H. M. Field, *The Life of David Dudley Field* (1898).

14. James Kent (1763–1847) was appointed a justice of the New York Supreme Court in 1798, became chief justice in 1804 and chancellor of the Court of Chancery in 1814, holding that post until his retirement in 1823. The sixth edition of his *Commentaries,* which he had prepared, was published in 1848. The twelfth edition by Holmes, referred to in the text, contained elaborate analytical and critical notes by Holmes. Holmes himself had no great admiration for Kent. In a letter to John Norton Pomeroy (May 22, 1872) Holmes commented: "I . . . have to keep a civil tongue in my head while I am his [Kent's] valet—but his arrangement is chaotic—he

has no general ideas except wrong ones and his treatment of special topics is often confused to the last degree." Quoted in M. Howe, *Justice Oliver Wendell Holmes—The Proving Years (1870–1882)* 16 (1963).

15. On Story, see note 11 *supra*.

16. On the establishment of the National Reporter System, and its fateful consequences, see Chapter 3 *infra*, note 24 and the accompanying text.

17. The expansion of the admiralty jurisdiction during the pre–Civil War period is traced in outline in Chapter I of G. Gilmore and C. Black, *The Law of Admiralty* (2d ed. 1975). For a more detailed account see D. Robertson, *Admiralty and Federalism: History and Analysis of Problems of Federal-State Relations in the Maritime Law of the United States* (1970).

18. 41 U.S. (16 Pet.) 1 (1842). Justice Catron dissented on a minor point of negotiable instruments law but did not express disapproval of the main part of Story's majority opinion.

19. Which was to be held unconstitutional in Erie R. Co. v. Tompkins, 304 U.S. 64 (1938). The Erie case will be discussed in Chapter 4 *infra*, text following note 52.

20. 5 Johns. Ch. Rep. 54 (1821); aff'd 20 Johns. 637 (1822).

21. For example, Wheaton v. Peters, 33 U.S. (8 Pet.) 591 (1834), digested note 4 *supra*, in which Story had concurred with McLean's opinion for the Court. For the ambiguous and possibly discreditable role that Story may have played in the Wheaton case, see Dunne, note 11 *supra*, 323 *et seq.*

22. See note 3 *supra* and the accompanying text for the argument, advanced by Crosskey, that this had indeed been the original intent of the framers of the federal Constitution. However, nothing in Story's opinion suggests that any of the Justices thought that the Court in Swift was returning to a true faith which had been temporarily forgotten. Crosskey naturally approved of Swift v. Tyson (and deplored the Erie case, note 19 *supra*). See 2 Crosskey, *Politics and the Constitution in the History of the United States*, Chapters XXV, XXVI (1953). Crosskey rehearses the long series of cases (including Wheaton v. Peters) which Story could have cited (but did not cite) in Swift v. Tyson (which Crosskey discusses at p. 856 *et seq.*). Crosskey's suggestion is that Story ignored the earlier cases in order to avoid embarrassment for the Court and perhaps in order to avoid

"unduly" prolonging his opinion (the latter suggestion being less than persuasive, given the length of a typical opinion by Story).

23. See Carlisle v. Wishart, 11 Ohio 172 (1842), which involved the same question (whether antecedent debt constituted value for the purpose of cutting off defenses) decided in Swift v. Tyson. The Ohio Court, overruling an earlier decision of its own, followed Swift v. Tyson, commenting that "[I]n a country like ours, where so much communication and interchange exists between the different members of the confederacy, to preserve uniformity in the great principles of commercial law, is of much interest to the mercantile world." Quoted in 2 Crosskey, note 22 *supra*, at p. 856.

24. Examples, drawn from my own field, of controverted issues for which the Supreme Court proposed solutions which promptly became the law of the land both in federal and state courts would include: (1) rights of bondholders under railroad and industrial mortgages to property acquired after the execution of the mortgage (Pennock v. Coe, 64 U.S. (23 How.) 117 (1859); United States v. New Orleans R.R. 79 U.S. (12 Wall.) 362 (1870); see 2 G. Gilmore, *Security Interests in Personal Property* §28.1 (1965)); (2) right of buyer of goods to reject because of trivial defects in seller's tender— the so-called "perfect tender" rule (Norrington v. Wright, 115 U.S. 188 (1885); Filley v. Pope, 115 U.S. 213 (1885)); (3) right to bring action for anticipatory breach of contract (i.e. repudiation before the time scheduled for performance) (Roehm v. Horst, 178 U.S. 1 (1899). In Robinson v. Elliott, 89 U.S. (22 Wall.) 513 (1874) the Court attempted, but failed, to solve a long-standing controversy about the validity of so-called stock-in-trade mortgages under which the mortgagor retained the right to sell the mortgaged goods (see discussion in 1 G. Gilmore, *op. cit. supra*, §2.5). In most of its late nineteenth-century cases of this type, of which there were a great many, the Court did not emphasize the fact that it was proposing (or, in a term which has a current vogue, "fashioning") a "federal rule"; indeed the typical opinion in such cases does not even cite Swift v. Tyson. The Justice who is writing for the Court takes note of the controversy which has arisen, reviews the arguments on both sides, cites authorities not only from state and federal courts in this country but from England and occasionally the civil law countries, and thus arrives at the Court's decision (which in nine cases out of ten was unanimous). The cases through this period, at least at the Supreme Court level, were entirely faithful to the spirit of Story's

Swift v. Tyson opinion, which is described in the following paragraph of the text.

25. De Tocqueville (1805–1859) visited the United States in 1831 and 1832. The first volume of his *De la Démocratie en Amérique* was published in 1835; the second volume in 1840. The first English translation by Henry Reeve was published in three volumes between 1835 and 1840.

26. In the following discussion I have borrowed heavily from R. Cover, *Justice Accused: Antislavery and the Judicial Process* (1975). The idea that the moral pressures to which antislavery judges were subjected when they were required to decide slavery cases drove them to adopt the techniques of legal formalism is entirely Professor Cover's. He is not of course responsible for the use I have made of his idea.

27. As has recently been argued by R. Fogel and S. Engerman, *Time on the Cross* (1974) who purport to prove, with a wealth of statistical data, that in the United States in 1860 slave labor in the Southern states was more productive and more efficient than free labor in the Northern states.

28. Lemuel Shaw (1781–1861) served as chief justice of the Supreme Judicial Court of Massachusetts from 1830 to 1860. On Shaw see L. Levy, *The Law of the Commonwealth and Chief Justice Shaw* (1957).

29. See Story's opinion in Prigg v. Pennsylvania, 41 U.S. (16 Pet.) 539 (1842); Shaw's opinion in Thomas Sims's Case, 61 Mass. (7 Cush.) 285 (1851). In the Prigg case the defendant, an agent for a Maryland slave owner, had, without the aid of legal process, apprehended alleged fugitive slaves in Pennsylvania and returned them to Maryland. He was convicted in Pennsylvania for violation of the state kidnapping statute. In the Supreme Court of the United States, the conviction was reversed (McLean, J., dissenting) on the ground that the Pennsylvania statute was unconstitutional as applied to Prigg. Seven separate opinions were filed in the Supreme Court (an unheard of performance for the time). Story's opinion, which came to be considered the leading opinion, emphasized the exclusivity of federal power under Article IV of the federal Constitution and the Fugitive Slave Act of 1793. Sims's case involved the Fugitive Slave Act of 1850, which provided for the appointment of federal commissioners empowered to order the return of alleged fugitives (whose own testimony was not admissible in the proceedings), without

appeal to the courts. Sims was apprehended as a fugitive in Boston and an application was made to Shaw, as chief justice of the Massachusetts Court, for a writ of habeas corpus. Shaw refused to issue the writ, concluding in his opinion that the Act of 1850 was in all respects constitutional. Shaw was involved in several other fugitive slave proceedings, in all of which he consistently maintained the power of the federal authorities, but Sims's case was the only one in which he wrote an opinion. On the opinions by Story and Shaw, see Cover, note 26 *supra*. Levy, note 28 *supra*, Chapter 6, discusses Shaw's involvement in the Sims case and other fugitive slave cases.

30. Cover, note 26 *supra*, after having reviewed the slavery opinions of the antislavery judges, turns in Part III of his book to what he calls "the moral-formal dilemma." He comments (at p. 199): "Whenever judges confronted the moral-formal dilemma they almost uniformly applied the legal rules. . . . Furthermore . . . these judges accompanied their decisions with striking manifestations of at least one of three related responsibility-mitigation mechanisms: (1) Elevation of the formal stakes (sometimes combined with minimization of the moral stakes). (2) Retreat to a mechanistic formalism. (3) Ascription of responsibility elsewhere."

31. That future will be the principal subject of the following Chapter 3.

32. K. Llewellyn, *The Common Law Tradition: Deciding Appeals* 45, note 40 (1960): "Apart from our early nineteenth century, I have come across the Grand Style only twice: in Cheyenne Indian law and in the classical Roman period." Llewellyn's odd reference to Cheyenne Indian law is explained by the fact that, in collaboration with an anthropologist, he had spent several years studying the law of the Cheyennes. The resulting book, Llewellyn and Hoebel, *The Cheyenne Way* (1941) makes fascinating reading. Llewellyn's paeans of praise for the techniques which the Cheyennes (before their confinement to a reservation in the late nineteenth century) had developed for settling disputes between members of the tribe may well reflect a romantic attachment for their once free way of life. We will not further inquire into Cheyenne law.

CHAPTER 3

1. On Langdell (1826–1906) and his deanship (1870–1895), see Chapter VI ("The Langdell Era") of A. Sutherland, *The Law at*

Harvard (1967). Professor Sutherland would not, of course, agree with my estimate of Langdell nor, presumably, with that of Professor Robert Stevens in his article cited Chapter 2 *supra*, note 1.

2. The quotation is from an address to the Harvard Law School Association in 1886, quoted by Sutherland, note 1 *supra*, at p. 175. For a contemporary echo of Dean Langdell's formulation, see Chapter 5 *infra*, note 11.

3. From the preface to Langdell's *Cases on Contracts* (1871), quoted by Sutherland, note 1 *supra*, at p. 174. Langdell's chief innovation in legal education was the introduction of the so-called case method of teaching in which the principal (in Langdell's original version, the only) materials presented to the student are the reports of decided cases, whose meaning is to be worked out by study and in classroom discussion. The case method, which was bitterly attacked for a generation after Langdell had introduced it, had, by the time of World War I, been adopted in almost all American law schools. Langdell's *Cases on Contracts* was the first casebook of all. Langdell's *Summary of the Law of Contracts* (which appeared as an appendix to the second edition of the casebook and was also published separately (1880)) is essentially a guide to the casebook, explaining which cases are "right" and which are "wrong." For more on Langdell's version of the case method, see the text at and following note 11 *infra*.

4. On the early developments, see S.F.C. Milsom, *Historical Foundations of the Common Law* (1969). For a brief but perceptive account of the slow emergence of the contract idea from the twelfth century to the nineteenth, see the essay by Professor Kessler ("From Status to Contract") which appears as Chapter I of F. Kessler and G. Gilmore, *Contracts: Cases and Materials* (2d ed. 1970).

5. Powell, *Essay upon the Law of Contracts and Agreements* (Dublin, 1790), may have been the first.

6. W. W. Story, *Treatise on the Law of Contracts not under Seal* (1844); a revised and expanded edition appeared in 1847. The author, William Wetmore Story, was Justice Joseph Story's son.

7. The list in the text is taken from the "Advertisement" to the second edition of Story, note 6 *supra*.

8. I have given my own analysis of the late nineteenth-century general theory of contract in Chapters I and II of *The Death of*

Contract (1974), a book which has not met with universal approval. On the critical reaction to the book, see Chapter 5 *infra*, note 9. Despite the book's many shortcomings, I have not been persuaded by my critics that my reconstruction was fundamentally in error.

9. Consider, for example, the title of an American book published in 1889, J. Bishop, *Commentaries on the Non-Contract Law and especially as to Common Affairs not of Contract or the Every-Day Rights and Torts*. The first American treatise to use the word in its title was Hilliard, *The Law of Torts, or Private Wrongs* (1859); the first English treatise on torts, Addison, *Wrongs and Their Remedies*, appeared in 1860. Bishop (at p. 2, note 1) quotes Sir Frederick Pollock as referring to a "a meagre and unthinking digest of 'The Law of Actions on the Case for Torts and Wrongs,' published in 1720, remarkable chiefly for the depths of historical ignorance which it occasionally reveals." Bishop has an amusing footnote (at p. 2, note 2) on the refusal of American law book publishers in the 1850s even to consider a book on such an outlandish subject. He quotes himself as having remarked to a friend while they were watching a streetcleaner at work: "Well, when I become too demented to swing a broom, I am going to set up in business as a great law publisher."

10. "Trespass" and "case" have already been identified, text following note 4 *supra*. "Conversion" means the wrongful taking or detention of another's property. The other terms are self-explanatory.

11. From the preface to Langdell's *Cases on Contracts* (1871), quoted by Sutherland, note 1 *supra*, at p. 174. On Langdell's introduction of the case method of teaching law, see note 3 *supra*.

12. For a few examples of the major surgery, drawn from the contract area, see *The Death of Contract*, note 8 *supra*, at p. 22 *et seq.*

13. Oliver Wendell Holmes, Jr. (1841-1935), who served on the Supreme Judicial Court of Massachusetts from 1883 to 1903 and on the Supreme Court of the United States from 1903 until his retirement in 1933, is the most celebrated figure in American jurisprudence. By far the best study of Holmes's early life and pre-judicial career are the two volumes by the late Mark De Wolfe Howe, *The Shaping Years: 1841-1870* (1957); *The Proving Years: 1870-1882* (1963). Howe's second volume, *The Proving Years*,

analyzes Holmes's 1881 book, *The Common Law*, which will presently be discussed in the text. Howe also wrote a perceptive introduction to *The Common Law* in his 1963 edition of that book. To avoid misunderstanding, I should add that I have, for some years, been engaged in preparing a book on Holmes's judicial career, which will be a sequel to the two Howe volumes. What I shall have to say about Holmes and his ideas in the following discussion derives from the work I have done on that book. I have analyzed Holmes's contribution to contract theory in *The Death of Contract* (1974), note 8 *supra*. Some reviewers seem to have taken—I would say, mistaken—my discussion as an attack on Holmes. It may be that some admirers of Holmes will take the following discussion in the same way. It is surely true that my Holmes has little in common with the Holmes of popular myth and legend. Holmes, to the extent that I can follow the dark outlines of his thought, seems to me to have been both a greater man and a more profound thinker than the mythical Holmes ever was.

14. A good place in which to observe the elaboration of the myth is the volumes of Herbert Croly's *New Republic*. Holmes, a great letter writer in his old age, carried on correspondences with both Laski and Frankfurter over many years. The Holmes-Laski correspondence (edited by Howe) was published as the *Holmes-Laski Letters: the Correspondence of Mr. Justice Holmes and Harold J. Laski, 1916–1935* (1953). The Holmes-Frankfurter correspondence has not been published.

15. *The Common Law* 38 (Howe ed. 1963).

16. *Id.* at p. 36.

17. On Peirce (1839–1914) see Young, "Charles Sanders Peirce" in *Studies in the Philosophy of Charles Sanders Peirce* (Weiner and Young eds. 1952); P. Weiss, Biography of Charles S. Peirce, 14 *Dict. of American Biography* 398 (1934), reprinted in *Perspectives on Peirce* 1 (R. Bernstein ed. 1965). On the parallelism between the ideas of Holmes and Peirce, see Note, "Holmes, Peirce and Legal Pragmatism," 84 *Yale L.J.* 1123 (1975) (by J. D. Miller).

18. For what Holmes thought of Kent, see Chapter 2 *supra*, note 14.

19. When the lectures were published, Holmes added a cryptic preface, less than a page long, which ends: "If, within the bounds which I have set myself, any one should feel inclined to reproach

me for a want of greater detail, I can only quote the words of Lehuërou, 'Nous faisons une théorie et non un spicilège.'" Even buffs of nineteenth-century historiography may find themselves defeated by Lehuërou, just as those familiar with the French language may be baffled by "spicilège." Lehuërou, a Belgian historian who flourished in the first half of the nineteenth century, wrote, among other things, a history of the Merovingian Kings. "Spicilège" (L. spicilegium) originally referred to the remnants that can be gleaned from a field after the principal harvest has been completed. By analogical extension, it came to be used to refer to the publication of historical trivia after the main outlines of a period have become known. Perhaps Holmes threw in this mysterious, indeed almost incomprehensible quotation as a way of alerting the astute reader that what was to be taken seriously in the book was the theory, not the historical details. I do not know from what work Holmes took the quotation. I am by no means the first to advance the proposition that *The Common Law* was a work of theoretical speculation, not of history. Mark De Wolfe Howe commented, in his introduction to his 1963 edition (at p. xx): "*The Common Law* is not primarily a work of legal history. It is an endeavor in philosophy—a speculative undertaking in which the author sought to find in the materials of legal history data which would support a new interpretation of the legal order."

20. *The Common Law* 32 (Howe ed. 1963).

21. At the beginning of the fourth lecture ("Fraud, Malice, and Intent—The Theory of Torts") Holmes briefly summarized what he had already said in his second lecture ("The Criminal Law") and continued: "It remains to be seen whether a similar reduction is possible on the civil side of the law, and whether thus fraudulent, malicious, intentional, and negligent wrongs can be brought into a philosophically continuous series." *The Common Law* 104 (Howe ed. 1963). The answer to Holmes's query was, as it hardly needs saying: Yes.

The discussion in the text draws on an unpublished paper by Charles Yablon, Esq., Yale Law School, Class of 1976.

22. *The Common Law* 76, 77 (Howe ed. 1963).

23. On the American law school, see R. Stevens, "Two Cheers for 1870," cited in Chapter 2 *supra*, note 1. On the Harvard Law School, see A. Sutherland, *The Law at Harvard* (1967).

24. As originally established (between 1879 and 1887) the Reporter System included the reports of all state courts of last resort as well as the reports of the Supreme Court of the United States and the reports of some but not all the cases decided by the inferior federal courts. Beginning in 1888 the coverage of the New York reports was extended to include cases decided in the lower courts of the state (a distinction which was also conferred on the California reports, but not until 1959).

25. See text at note 11 *supra*.

26. See K. Llewellyn, *The Common Law Tradition: Deciding Appeals* (1960); *cf.* Chapter 1, note 11 *supra* and the accompanying text. L. Friedman, *A History of American Law* 334 (1973), seems to concur: "Many appellate opinions of the '80's and '90's are torture to read—bombastic, diffuse, labored, drearily logical, crammed with unnecessary citations."

27. See Chapter 2 *supra*, text at and following note 18.

28. The Supreme Court of the United States approved the practice of appointing receivers in Covington Drawbridge Co. v. Shephard, 62 U.S. (21 How.) 112 (1858) (tolls on a bridge); in Davis v. Gray, 83 U.S. (16 Wall.) 203, 220 (1872) Justice Swayne upheld the appointment of receivers for insolvent railroads "to operate such roads, until the difficulties are removed, or such arrangements are made that the roads can be sold with the least sacrifice of the interests of those concerned." On the history of the equity receivership, see 6 *Collier on Bankruptcy* §0.04 (14th ed., revised 1972).

29. On Erie R. Co. v. Tompkins, 304 U.S. 64 (1938), which held that the doctrine of Swift v. Tyson was (and always had been) unconstitutional, see Chapter 4 *infra*, text following note 52.

30. John Bannister Gibson (1780–1853) was chief justice of the Supreme Court of Pennsylvania from 1827 until his death; on Shaw, see Chapter 2 *supra*, note 28; on Kent, see Chapter 2 *supra*, note 14.

31. It has been pointed out to me that there are statutes that break new ground or authorize the creation of new institutions (corporations, administrative agencies, authorities of all kinds) and thus can hardly be considered as being in derogation of the past. The point is obviously well taken. The statement in the text refers to the general run of statutes which regulate civil liability.

32. *Stare decisis* (to stand by the decisions) is conventional legal shorthand for the idea that a court is bound, in deciding a current

case, to follow its own past decisions in "like" cases. Which current cases are "like" which past cases is a point on which opposing counsel tend to disagree.

33. On the invalidation of social legislation by the state courts during the second half of the nineteenth century, see L. Friedman, *A History of American Law* 311 *et seq.* (1973). Two examples of the "freedom of contract" approach are Godcharles v. Wigeman, 113 Pa. St. 431, 6 Atl. 354 (1886) and Ritchie v. People, 115 Ill. 98, 40 N.E. 454 (1895). In the Godcharles case the Pennsylvania Court held unconstitutional a statute which required certain mining and manufacturing businesses to pay their employees at least once a month and to pay in cash or legal tender, not in scrip redeemable only at company stores, and it forbade overcharging at such stores (an attempt, said the Court, speaking of the statute as a whole, "to do what, in this country, cannot be done, that is, prevent persons who are *sui juris* from making their own contracts"). In the Ritchie case the Illinois Court, which had a long series of cases of this sort to its credit, invalidated a statute which restricted to eight hours a day and forty-eight hours a week the work of women in factories and "workshops" (a "purely arbitrary restriction upon the fundamental rights of the citizen to control his or her own time and faculties"). I have borrowed these examples from Professor Friedman's discussion, cited above. As late as 1911 the New York Court of Appeals invalidated a Workmen's Compensation Act which the legislature had enacted the previous year, Ives v. South Buffalo Ry. Co., 200 N.Y. 271, 94 N.E. 431 (1911). Professor Friedman makes the point that not all state courts shared the views of the Pennsylvania and Illinois courts, even in the 1880s and 1890s. By the time of World War I most courts had abandoned the extreme position illustrated by the cases which have been cited in this note. Note 36 *infra* discusses other cases of this type which were made notable by the dissents of Holmes, J. In the Supreme Court the conservative majority precipitated a constitutional crisis by its repeated invalidation of New Deal legislation in the early 1930s—a crisis which was eventually resolved, after the failure of President Roosevelt's court-packing plan, by changes in the Court's membership. The crisis, while it endured, called forth attacks by liberals on the entire institution of judicial review of legislative action; see, e.g., E. Corwin, *The Twilight of the Supreme Court* (1934); *Court over Constitution* (1938).

34. On these matters, see Chapter 2 *supra*.

35. Kessler, "Contracts of Adhesion—Some Thoughts about Freedom of Contract," 43 *Colum. L. Rev.* 629 (1943) may have been the first expression of this idea in the American literature. It seems to have become commonplace in the 1960s. See, among many examples which could be cited, L. Friedman, *Contract Law in America* 20–24 (1965); Farnsworth, "Legal Remedies for Breach of Contract," 70 *Colum. L. Rev.* 1145, 1216 (1970); G. Gilmore, *The Death of Contract* 94 *et seq.* (1974). For an example from England, Atiyah, *An Introduction to the Law of Contract* 3 (2d ed. 1971). Among commentators who can be identified as liberals on the political spectrum, the parallelism between late nineteenth-century legal and economic theories is stressed to make the point that, in the late twentieth century, neither the legal nor the economic theory seems plausible. Conservative commentators, accepting the parallelism, make the points that both laissez-faire economic theory and the legal structure which echoed it were (and are) sound and that, to the extent we have abandoned either, salvation lies in returning to the true faith. Professor Richard Posner of the University of Chicago Law School has been an influential spokesman for this point of view. See his "A Theory of Negligence," 1 *J. of Legal Studies* 29 (1972); also his book, *Economic Analysis of Law* (1973). For a critical review of the book, see Leff, "Economic Analysis of Law: Some Realism about Nominalism," 60 *Va. L. Rev.* 451 (1974).

36. See text at and following note 15 *supra*. See, among the many illustrations that could be put forward, Holmes's celebrated dissent in Lochner v. New York, 198 U.S. 45 (1905) in which the Court invalidated a New York statute which limited employment in bakeries to sixty hours a week and ten hours a day. The majority held that the statute was an arbitrary interference with the right of freedom to contract, guaranteed by the Fourteenth Amendment to the federal Constitution. Holmes, referring to the "right of a majority to embody their opinions in law," commented: "I think that the word liberty in the Fourteenth Amendment is perverted when it is held to prevent the natural outcome of a dominant opinion . . ." (At p. 76 of 198 U.S.) See also his dissent in Coppage v. Kansas, 236 U.S. 1, 26 (1914) in which the majority of the Court invalidated a Kansas statute which prohibited so-called yellow dog contracts (in which, as a condition of employment, workers were required to promise not to join a union). During his tenure on the

Massachusetts Court, the majority of the Court held, in Vegelahn
v. Guntner, 167 Mass. 92 (1896), that picketing by members of a
striking union was illegal, even though the picketing was not accompanied by violence or the threat of violence: Holmes dissented
in one of his most eloquent opinions, writing (at p. 108 of 167 Mass.):
"One of the eternal conflicts out of which life is made up is that
between the effort of every man to get the most he can for his services,
and that of society, disguised under the name of capital, to get his
services for the least possible return. Combination on the one side
is patent and powerful. Combination on the other is the necessary
and desirable counterpart, if the battle is to be carried on in a fair
and equal way." In his dissent in Coppage v. Kansas, Holmes cited
this passage of his dissent in Vegelahn v. Guntner. The Vegelahn
dissent earned Holmes a reputation as a radical. When President
Roosevelt nominated him for the Supreme Court in 1902, Holmes
feared that that reputation might jeopardize his chances for con-
firmation. See his letters to Pollock of August 13, 1902, and September 23, 1902, in 1 *Holmes-Pollock Letters* 103, 106 (Howe ed.
1961).

CHAPTER 4

1. "The Papacy is not other than the Ghost of the deceased
Roman Empire, sitting crowned upon the grave thereof." Hobbes,
Leviathan Part IV, at 47 (1651).
2. On the survival of the Langdellian spirit, see text at and following note 44 *infra*, and text following note 8 to Chapter 5.
3. Brandeis (1856–1941) went into practice in Boston following
his graduation from the Harvard Law School in 1878. His practice,
which was originally of a perfectly conventional nature, gradually
involved him, on a national scale, with the great social and political
problems of the day, and he became known as the most effective
advocate of liberal or progressive ideology. Nominated to the
Supreme Court by President Wilson in 1916, he was bitterly attacked
by conservatives in the Senate hearings, but his appointment was
eventually confirmed by a 47–22 vote. He served as an Associate
Justice until his retirement in 1939.
4. Pound (1870–1964) received a Ph.D. in botany from the
University of Nebraska in 1897 but never received a law degree,
although he had studied law at Harvard for a year (1889–1890). He

was admitted to the Nebraska bar and practiced law while teaching botany at the University of Nebraska. He was a professor of law at Harvard from 1910 to 1937 and served as dean from 1916 to 1936. For his advocacy of sociological jurisprudence, see his series of articles under the general title "The Scope and Purpose of Sociological Jurisprudence," 24 *Harv. L. Rev.* 591 (1912); 25 *id.* 140 (1912); 25 *id.* 489 (1912). The term "sociological jurisprudence," at that time, had little or nothing to do with the theories of academic sociologists; Pound and others used the term to mean an approach to law under which judges could and should weigh in the balance the social and economic consequences of their decisions. Thus he was one of the first to attack the premises of what I have called Langdellian jurisprudence (see Chapter 3 *supra*). The irony of Pound's overlong career was that, long before his death, he had come to be considered an arch-reactionary. In the 1930s he became the principal butt of the Legal Realists under circumstances which are described in note 25 *infra*.

5. On the Progressive Movement, see R. Wiebe, *Businessmen and Reform: A Study of the Progressive Movement* (1962); R. Wiebe, *The Search for Order, 1877–1920* (1967); S. Wood, *Constitutional Politics in the Progressive Era: Child Labor and the Law* (1968).

6. On the pre–Civil War codification movement, see Chapter 2 *supra*, text at and following note 9.

7. The Negotiable Instruments Law, universally nicknamed the N.I.L., was promulgated in 1896 and eventually enacted in all American jurisdictions. The Uniform Sales Act, which never acquired a nickname, was promulgated in 1906 and enacted in 37 states (the non-enacting states were mostly in the South and Southwest). Other commercial law statutes drafted during this period covered bills of lading, warehouse receipts, the transfer of share certificates, and conditional sales. All these statutes, including the N.I.L. and the Sales Act, were repealed in all enacting states when the Uniform Commercial Code was adopted. On the Code see §III of this chapter.

8. On Langdell and his ideas, see Chapter 3 *supra*.

9. On Swift v. Tyson, see Chapter 2 *supra*, text following note 18. Some examples of the nationally acceptable solutions which the device produced are collected in note 24 to Chapter 2.

10. Commissions to codify the common law (including the law

of contracts) were established by the Law Commissions Act 1965. Hahlo, in "Codifying the Common Law: Protracted Gestation," 38 *Mod. L. Rev.* 23, 26 (1975), commented that "the prospect of a codification of the law of contracts has receded into the nebulous future" and added that "Codes of the law of torts and the law of restitution lie unformed in the womb of time."

11. James Barr Ames (1846–1910) was appointed to the faculty of the Harvard Law School in 1873, became dean, succeeding Langdell, in 1895, and served in that office until shortly before his death. On Ames, see Chapter VII of A. Sutherland, *The Law at Harvard* (1967). Moot court arguments at the Harvard Law School are based on hypothetical cases which arise in the State of Ames (or, if a municipal ordinance is involved, in the City of Langdell). I do not know when the Harvards adopted this engaging practice but I know that it was in use in the 1960s.

12. S. Williston, *The Law Governing Sales of Goods at Common Law and under the Uniform Sales Act* (1909). The latest and, presumably, last edition of the sales treatise appeared, in four volumes, in 1948. The comment in the text is based on my own reading of the Sales Act case law while teaching the course on sales in several law schools over a good many years. Williston (1861–1963) was a member of the Harvard Law School faculty from 1890 to 1938. In addition to his treatise on sales he wrote a treatise on contracts which was first published in 1920. He was the Chief Reporter for the Restatement of Contracts; the Restatement project is discussed in the following passage of the text. Williston was one of the best statutory draftsmen who has ever worked at that mysterious art; he was the most ingenious system-builder in the history of our jurisprudence; he wrote with lucidity and grace.

13. The founder and guiding spirit of the Institute and the Restatement project was William Draper Lewis, dean of the University of Pennsylvania Law School. See Goodrich, "The Story of the American Law Institute," 1951 *Wash. U. L.Q.* 283. Judge Herbert Goodrich, the author of the article cited, succeeded Dean Lewis as director of the Institute.

14. See Chapter 1 *supra*, text following note 4.

15. Indeed the Restatements, which had apparently been conceived as formulations good for all time, endured, in their original

form, for not much more than a generation. Since the 1950s the American Law Institute has been at work producing a "Second Series" of Restatements. I have commented on some of the provisions of the (still unfinished) Second Restatement of Contracts in Chapter III, text following note 163, of *The Death of Contract* (1974).

16. Cardozo (1870–1938) studied law at Columbia and practiced in New York City from 1891 until he was elected to the New York Supreme Court in 1913. Promoted to the Court of Appeals (the court of last resort in the New York system) the following year, he served on that court until his appointment to the Supreme Court of the United States in 1932.

17. See, e.g., B. Shientag, *The Seventy-Fifth Anniversary of the Birth of Justice Benjamin N. Cardozo* 1–2 (1945): "What words are there to describe the charm of an uncommon gentleness, of a singular simplicity that goes with spiritual distinction; to picture that candor, that rare integrity and purity of mind, that life of intellectual opulence and moral fervor? What words have we to adumbrate that exquisite grace of humility, that abiding serenity, that intense tenderness and compassion which flowed from having himself suffered?"

18. See, e.g., Allegheny College v. National Chautauqua County Bank, 246 N.Y. 369, 379, 159 N.E. 173, 177 (1927) (Kellogg, J., dissenting); Jacob & Youngs, Inc. v. Kent, 230 N.Y. 239, 245, 129 N.E. 889, 892 (1921) (McLaughlin, J., dissenting); MacPherson v. Buick Motor Co., 217 N.Y. 382, 395, 111 N.E. 1050, 1055 (1916) (Bartlett, C. J., dissenting). The Allegheny College case involved the law of charitable subscriptions; Jacob and Youngs involved the so-called rule of substantial performance in construction contracts; the MacPherson case involved a manufacturer's liability to a remote buyer for a defectively manufactured product. In all three cases Cardozo, writing the majority opinions, imposed liability on defendants who would almost certainly (with the possible exception of the Allegheny College case) not have been held liable if anyone but Cardozo had been stating and analyzing the prior case law which the majority opinions purported to follow.

19. See, e.g., Comfort v. McCorkle, 149 Misc. 826, 268 N.Y.S. 192 (Sup. Ct. 1933). The plaintiff had suffered a fire loss. The defendant, agent of the insurance company with which plaintiff carried his fire insurance, promised the plaintiff that he (the agent)

would file proof of loss. No proof was filed within the required period and as a result the insurance company was discharged from liability on the policy. In an action against the agent, judgment was for the defendant. The result was not only a miscarriage of justice but also a completely unnecessary misreading of Cardozo's Allegheny College opinion, note 18 *supra*.

20. On *The Common Law*, see Chapter 3 *supra*, text following note 18. *The Nature of the Judicial Process* was published in 1921.

21. See note 4 *supra* for this use of the term "sociological jurisprudence" in the early part of the twentieth century.

22. *The Nature of the Judicial Process* 166–167 (1921).

23. Professor Arthur Corbin, who had been responsible for Cardozo's giving the lectures at Yale, wrote: "[Cardozo] was aware that his conception of the judicial process was not the generally accepted one; and he had a slight hesitation about the publication of his lectures. With a touch of humor, he remarked, 'If I were to publish them I would be impeached.' " Corbin, Foreword to B. Cardozo, *The Growth of the Law*, at vi (1966).

24. W. Twining, *Karl Llewellyn and the Realist Movement* (1973). Professor Twining devotes the first five chapters of his book, plus a concluding chapter, to the Realist Movement. On Llewellyn, see Chapter 1 *supra*, note 11.

25. The law review controversy stemmed from a short article by Dean Pound of Harvard which he entitled "The Call for a Realist Jurisprudence," 44 *Harv. L. Rev.* 697 (1931). The issue of the *Law Review* in which the article appeared was dedicated to Justice Holmes, as a tribute to him on his ninetieth birthday. Pound had promised the editors a piece for their Holmes issue but had not had time to prepare one and gave them the piece on Realist Jurisprudence (which is the only item not related to Holmes in the entire issue) as a substitute. It is about fifteen pages long, has no footnotes, and shows every sign of having been hastily written (or perhaps dictated). Pound, after briefly mentioning the nineteenth-century schools of historical and analytical jurisprudence and the twentieth-century school of sociological jurisprudence with which he himself had been associated (see note 4 *supra*), said that a new school, which he called Realist Jurisprudence, seemed to be establishing itself. Without naming any of the members of the new "school," he then proceeded to a not unsympathetic analysis of what he identified as five principal characteristics of their writing.

Karl Llewellyn and Jerome Frank felt themselves to be the targets of what they regarded as Dean Pound's attack. Llewellyn, the previous year, had published an article which he called "A Realistic Jurisprudence—The Next Step," 30 *Colum. L. Rev.* 431 (1930), in the course of which he had made some less than flattering remarks about Pound. Frank may have felt that his recently published *Law and the Modern Mind* (1930) was what Pound was getting at. At all events Llewellyn and Frank jointly prepared a reply to Pound which was published, under Llewellyn's name, as "Some Realism about Realism—Responding to Dean Pound," 44 *Harv. L. Rev.* 1222 (1931). Identifying themselves (and a number of others) as "Realists," they argued, vehemently and at length, that Pound had totally misconceived what they had been saying and that none of Pound's five "characteristics" could be properly applied to their work. They ended by denying that there was anything that could be properly described as a "school" of realist jurisprudence—which seemed inconsistent with their identification of themselves as Realists.

The absurd truth appears to be that Pound had not had either Llewellyn or Frank in mind; it is entirely possible that he had never read anything by either of them. Thus it was quite true that his five "characteristics" had only an accidental or remote application to the work of Llewellyn or Frank (or most of the other people whom they co-opted as "Realists"). In his hastily written piece Pound was, in all probability, commenting on trends he had noticed in recent legal writing without having any individual or group in mind. He was, apparently, mystified by their attack on him.

From this tissue of misunderstandings came the celebrated controversy about Legal Realism—which, before it had finally run its course in the late 1930s, accounted for hundreds, if not thousands, of tedious pages in the law reviews. The saddest part of the story is that Dean Pound, who had been one of the earliest and most effective spokesmen in the reaction against Langdellian formalism, ended up as the favorite whipping-boy of the new school (or non-school or anti-school). Thus the reputation of a man who had made a notable contribution to our jurisprudence was unfairly tarnished—which was a great loss to all of us, including the Realists themselves.

Professor Paul Freund, who was president of the *Harvard Law Review* when the Holmes issue was published in 1931, has confirmed the foregoing account of an exchange which he characterizes as having had a "sadly comic" quality.

26. Indeed Llewellyn was accustomed to describe his own writings as examples of what the new jurisprudence was about. In a note on "Realism and Method" in *The Common Law Tradition: Deciding Appeals* 508 *et seq.* (1960) he wrote (at p. 512): "I therefore claim to know what it ["Realistic jurisprudence"] was about and what it is about. I now put forward, explicitly as a proper product and exhibit of *real* realism, this book." (Emphasis in original.) In 1960 Llewellyn read a draft of a piece of mine which appeared as "Legal Realism: Its Cause and Cure," 70 *Yale L.J.* 1037 (1961). He commented: "Where you all go wrong is in thinking that Realism was a theory. It was not. It was merely a methodology."

27. See Chapter 3 *supra*, text at and following note 2.

28. Arthur Linton Corbin (1874–1967) took his law degree at Yale and then practiced law briefly in Cripple Creek, Colorado. He spent the rest of his career teaching law at Yale. He published many law review articles on the law of contracts; his treatise on contracts appeared in 1950. I am on record as having described the Corbin treatise as "the greatest law book ever written" (*The Death of Contract* 57 (1974)). I was Professor Corbin's student and later, as a junior member of the Yale faculty, benefited greatly from his wise counsel.

29. The first edition of Williston's treatise, *The Law of Contracts*, appeared in 1920. On the relationship between Corbin and Williston, see Corbin, "Samuel Williston," 76 *Harv. L. Rev.* 1327 (1963), a moving tribute written after Williston's death when Corbin himself was almost ninety. On Williston, see note 12 *supra*.

30. 1 A. Corbin, *Contracts* §110, at 494 (1963): "In each new case, the question for the court is 'should this promise be enforced.' Its problem is not merely to determine mechanically, or logically, whether it falls within Professor Wiseacre's statement of the doctrine of consideration or complies with some commonly repeated definition. This is not to say that the Professor's statement, or Restatement, or the learned judge's dictum, can be safely disregarded."

There can be no doubt that "Professor Wiseacre" was Williston. I assume that the "learned judge" was Holmes.

On the battle between Corbin and Williston over the definition of "consideration" to be adopted in the Restatement of Contracts, see my discussion in *The Death of Contract* 62 *et seq.* (1974).

31. Wesley Alba Sturges (1893–1962) took his law degree at

Columbia and spent most of his professional career teaching at the Yale Law School, serving as dean 1945–1954. By way of explaining why his students revered him, I will retell an anecdote which I used in an obituary piece which I called "For Wesley Sturges: On the Teaching and Study of Law," 72 *Yale L.J.* 646 (1963). In the fall of 1941 a number of students (of whom I was one) came to the odd conclusion that our legal education would not be complete without a course in the common law forms of action—a subject which, then as now, did not make the grade in the forward-looking curriculum of the Yale Law School. I quote from 72 *Yale L.J.* at pp. 646, 654: "We decided to ask Wesley Sturges to offer such a course in the spring term. When our delegation waited on him his attitude was one of grave courtesy and mild amusement: he neither commended us for our historical interest, nor castigated us for having lost touch with reality. He would, he said, offer the course if a sufficient number of students signed up. He did not point out to us that, in addition to his having a full teaching schedule for the spring term, he had committed a large portion of his time to activities on behalf of both the state and federal governments in connection with what was called, before Pearl Harbor, the defense effort. The course was announced, about twenty students signed up and, through the catastrophic spring of 1942, Wesley labored patiently with us as we canvased the mysteries of replevin, trover, detinue, and debt. . . . What did Wesley teach us? He taught us, in a way that none of us will ever forget, something—indeed a great deal—about the use and the uses of words. I can think of few things that are more central to the lawyer's craft and art. He taught us to be forever on our guard against the slippery generality, the received principle, the authoritative proposition. He taught us to trust no one's judgment except our own—and not to be too sure of that. He taught us how to live by our wits. He taught us, in a word, how to be lawyers."

32. Sturges, "Legal Theory and Real Property Mortgages," 37 *Yale L.J.* 691 (1928). I discussed the article in the obituary piece, note 31 *supra*, 72 *Yale L.J.* at p. 651 *et seq.*

33. W. Sturges, *The Law of Credit Transactions* (1930).

34. Nothing, that is, on conventional law or legal theory. He became interested in arbitration as a promising alternative to judicial adjudication and published a comprehensive treatise on that subject, W. Sturges, *A Treatise on Commercial Arbitrations and Awards* (1930).

35. On Llewellyn, see Chapter 1 *supra*, note 11; on Llewellyn and Legal Realism, see note 25 *supra* and the accompanying text. On pre-Langdellian pluralism, see Chapter 3 *supra*, text following note 6. For another example of the return toward pluralism during this period, see Kessler, "Contracts of Adhesion—Some Thoughts about Freedom of Contract," 43 *Colum. L. Rev.* 629 (1943), which I have discussed in a tribute to Kessler, 84 *Yale L.J.* 672 (1975).

36. See "On Warranty of Quality, and Society," 36 *Colum. L. Rev.* 699 (1936), 37 *id.* 341 (1937); "Through Title to Contract and a Bit Beyond," 3 *Law—A Century of Progress* 80 (1937), reprinted 15 *N.Y.U. L.Q. Rev.* 159 (1938); "Across Sales on Horseback," 52 *Harv. L. Rev.* 725 (1939). The casebook, *Cases and Materials on Sales* (1930), was not a success in the academic marketplace and never appeared in a second edition. I have been told that it was "unteachable" (except, of course, when Llewellyn was doing the teaching). However, in the late 1940s it was the indispensable reference tool for any young instructor assigned to teach the sales course. I know it was for me.

37. On what Holmes meant by a "philosophically continuous series," see Chapter 3 *supra*, text at note 21.

38. On the genesis of the Code project, see W. Twining, *Karl Llewellyn and the Realist Movement* (1973). Drafting on what became the Code started in the late 1930s. I became a member of the drafting staff in 1946 and served until the staff was disbanded in 1954. I subsequently served as a member of or as a consultant to committees charged with considering revisions of Article 9 (on Secured Transactions). The following discussion of the Code is based on my own memory of what went on.

Danzig's "A Comment on the Jurisprudence of the Uniform Commercial Code," 27 *Stan. L. Rev.* 621 (1975), is an interesting attempt to relate Llewellyn's jurisprudential ideas, as he expressed them in *The Common Law Tradition: Deciding Appeals* (1960), with the style and substance of the Code (particularly Article 2 on Sales). Professor Danzig emphasizes the open-endedness of the Code's drafting (i.e., the frequent use of such undefined and undefinable terms as "commercial reasonableness," "good faith," and so on). In the following discussion in the text I refer to Llewellyn's concept of a "case law code," which would abolish the past without attempting to control the future. That concept seems to be the same one that

Professor Danzig identifies in his comments on the Article 2 drafting. Professor Danzig, who appears to disapprove of this open-ended style of drafting, is, I believe, correct in drawing attention to the extent to which the style survived even in the final draft of Article 2. If he had included other articles of the Code (particularly Article 9 on Secured Transactions) in his analysis, he would, I am quite sure, have found much less open-endedness to complain about. By the time Article 9 was drafted the proponents of a much tighter style of drafting had taken charge. On the subsequent history of Article 9, see note 56 *infra*.

39. On the earlier codification of commercial law, see text following note 6 *supra*.

40. On the Restatements, see text at and following note 13 *supra*.

41. In the 1920s he had drafted for the Conference a Uniform Chattel Mortgage Act which, despite much merit, was not enacted anywhere. In the early 1930s he had drafted the Uniform Trust Receipts Act, which was widely enacted. On the Trust Receipts Act, see 1 G. Gilmore, *Security Interests in Personal Property*, Chapter 7 (1965).

42. On post–World War II judicial activism, see §V *infra*. The products liability cases, discussed in note 48 *infra* as an example of activism on the state court level in a private law area, effectively nullified the apparent victory of the conservatives in procuring the deletion of the proposed Code provisions which would have increased the liability of manufacturers for defective goods.

43. I was a law student myself in the early 1940s. I testify to what I witnessed.

44. The thesis of Carl Becker, *The Heavenly City of the Eighteenth-Century Philosophers* (1931), is that, despite their rhetorical attacks on church and state, Voltaire and the other "philosophes" in effect accepted the basic tenets of the ideology which they professed to despise. If I am right, the Realists and the Langdellians also shared a community of interest. See my comments, text at and following note 1 *supra*.

45. See Chapter 3 *supra*, text at note 2.

46. See Lasswell and McDougal, "Legal Education and Public Policy: Professional Training in the Public Interest," 52 *Yale L.J.* 203 (1943); McDougal, "The Law School of the Future: From Legal Realism to Policy Science in the World Community," 56 *Yale L.J.*

1345 (1947). After World War II Professor McDougal, whose initial field of specialization had been property law, turned to international law. With various collaborators he has produced a series of volumes on international law subjects in which he applies the theoretical insights on which his policy science system is based.

47. On the Progressive Movement, see note 5 *supra*.

48. On the Supreme Court itself the formation of a usually reliable activist majority for which Justices Black and Douglas were frequently the spokesmen dates from the 1940s. See the discussion in the text following note 53 *infra* of the growth of what has been called the New Federalism. One area in which that majority completely rewrote the law during the 1940s was that of recovery for death and injury for seamen and other maritime workers, see G. Gilmore and C. Black, *The Law of Admiralty*, 272 *et seq.* (2d ed. 1975). The most dramatic example of activism on the state court level in a private law field since World War II has been the imposition of "strict" (or no-fault) liability on manufacturers toward those who may be injured by the use of defective products. The strict liability idea, in whose formulation the California Supreme Court played a pioneering role (see Greenman v. Yuba Power Products, Inc., 59 Cal. 2d 57, 377 P. 2d 897 (1962)), had, in less than ten years, been widely adopted throughout the country and was accepted in §402A of the Second Restatement of Torts. On the products liability cases, which have generated an enormous literature, see the symposium "Products Liability: Economic Analysis and the Law," 38 *U. of Chi. L. Rev.* 1 (1970), in which the strict liability idea is attacked by some economists and lawyers but defended by others (including myself).

49. I do not mean that judicial activism will necessarily be our permanent state. See the discussion of what has been called the New Conceptualism in Chapter 5 *infra*, text following note 7.

50. See Chapter 3 *supra*, text following note 30.

51. I have traced this process in the area of contract law in Chapters III and IV of *The Death of Contract* (1974).

52. Erie R.R. v. Tompkins, 304 U.S. 64 (1938), per Brandeis, J. On Swift v. Tyson, see Chapter 2 *supra*, text following note 18. On the decline of the Swift v. Tyson device, see Chapter 3 *supra*, text following note 28.

53. One of the earliest discussions of the post-*Erie* federalization was in Judge Henry Friendly's 1964 Cardozo lecture to the Associa-

tion of the Bar of the City of New York, "In Praise of *Erie*—and of the New Federal Common Law," reprinted 39 *N.Y.U. L. Rev.* 383 (1964). For a review of the process in various fields, see 1 G. Gilmore, *Security Interests in Personal Property*, Chapter 13 (1965).

54. The federal supremacy idea received its most extensive development in the maritime injury and death cases, starting with Garrett v. Moore-McCormack Co., Inc., 317 U.S. 239 (1942). The long sequence of Supreme Court admiralty cases of this type is discussed in G. Gilmore and C. Black, *The Law of Admiralty*, §6–59 *et seq.* (2d ed. 1975). When a court talks of fashioning a federal rule where none previously existed, what is usually meant is that the court is choosing between conflicting rules which have established themselves on the state level or (as the Supreme Court used to do in the nineteenth century under Swift v. Tyson) arriving at a new synthesis derived from the conflicting rules. That is, the rule-fashioning process uses existing materials or recombines them; almost never is the new federal rule a radical departure.

55. Although, in the early days, the state courts did in fact adopt the federal rule more often than not. For an example, see Chapter 2 *supra*, note 23.

56. See my comments on the drafting history of the Uniform Commercial Code, text at and following note 42 *supra*. Indeed the tensions revealed by the developing case law under Article 9 of the Code (Secured Transactions) had become so acute by the late 1960s that the sponsoring organizations (see text at note 39 *supra*) undertook a revision of the article which was promulgated in 1972 and had, by 1976, been enacted in more than a dozen states. Thus we now have, and presumably will go on having, two versions of Article 9 in force—which is obviously destructive of the national uniformity in the law which the Code was designed to assure. Even so, the Article 9 story is a cause for rejoicing when we think of all the other statutes, state and federal, which are sorely in need of revision, have not been revised, and, in all probability, never will be revised.

57. Two celebrated examples of this process are the Elizabethan Statute of Fraudulent Conveyances (1570) and the Carolingian Statute of Frauds (1677). The dates of the statutes suggest how long the process takes.

58. The idea of this approach to the problem of statutory obsolescene was first suggested to me by a series of maritime industrial

accident cases which the Supreme Court of the United States decided during the 1950s and 1960s. These cases involved both the Jones Act (46 U.S.C. §688), a 1920 statute under which "seamen" (or their representatives) may recover for death or injury caused by "negligence" attributable to their employers, and the Longshoremen's and Harbor Workers' Compensation Act of 1927 (33 U.S.C. §901 *et seq.*), under which the employers of maritime workers (other than "seamen") were to be liable to their employees only for compensation under the act (and not for the damages recoverable in a tort action). By 1970 the Court had in effect nullified both the negligence requirement of the Jones Act and the exclusive liability provision of the Compensation Act; thus both seamen and other harbor workers could recover full damages without proving negligence. (1972 amendments to the Compensation Act were designed to overturn much of what the Court had done in the harbor worker cases.) For a full discussion of these developments, see G. Gilmore and C. Black, *The Law of Admiralty*, Chapter VI, particularly §6–56 (2d ed. 1975).

I wrote the passage in the text in 1974 with the maritime industrial accident cases in mind, speculating that state courts might well begin to treat the turn of the century Workmen's Compensation Acts in the same way that the Supreme Court had treated the federal act.

Since 1974 the California Supreme Court has provided a dramatic example of statutory nullification in Li v. Yellow Cab Co., 13 Cal. 3d 804, 119 Cal. Reptr. 858, 532 P. 2d 1226 (1975). The Court concluded that the California Civil Code of 1872 had adopted the common law contributory negligence rule (plaintiff's negligence, however slight, bars any recovery), took note of the fact that the California legislature had refused to amend the Code provision and held that, despite the Code, California would now adopt a "comparative negligence" rule (plaintiff's negligence will be taken into account in assessing damages but will not bar recovery). Courts in several other states have commented on the holding in the Li case without betraying any visible signs of shock or outrage.

59. As had been the case with the problem of statutory obsolescence (see note 59 *supra*), my attention was drawn to the problem of obsolete Supreme Court cases by some recent admiralty litigation. There are many areas of admiralty law in which the Supreme Court has not decided a case since the 1920s or even earlier, so that the

problem of obsolescence has become acute. See Petition of Chadade Steamship Co., Inc. (The Yarmouth Castle), 266 F. Supp. 517 (S.D. Fla. 1967) for a case in which, arguably, Judge Mehrtens, a highly respected admiralty judge, came "perilously close" to overruling (or refusing to follow) The Titanic, 233 U.S. 718 (1914). G. Gilmore and C. Black, *The Law of Admiralty*, 943–944 (2d ed. 1975).

Having reached this point in my own thinking, I was fascinated to come across a Note, "Lower Court Disavowal of Supreme Court Precedent," 60 *Va. L. Rev.* 494 (1974), which contains an elaborate, and excellent, discussion. The writer of the Note properly emphasizes, in addition to the problem of obsolescence, the problems created by the erosion of precedent during the period since the 1940s when the Supreme Court has been dominated, most of the time, by an activist majority. He also makes the interesting suggestion that the general decline in respect for precedent can be traced back to the Realist attack on formalism, citing White, "The Evolution of Reasoned Elaboration: Jurisprudential Criticism and Social Change," 59 *Va. L. Rev.* 279 (1973).

Evidently, these ideas are in the air. We shall, no doubt, hear more of them.

CHAPTER 5

1. See Chapter 1 *supra*, §II, where the eighteenth-century origins of the hypothesis are discussed.

2. See Chapter 4 *supra*, §IV.

3. The passage in the text is borrowed from "The Age of Antiquarius: On Legal History in a Time of Troubles," 39 *U. of Chi. L. Rev.* 475 (1972), a paper which I delivered as the inaugural William Winslow Crosskey Lecture in Legal History at the University of Chicago Law School.

4. I have been told that large law firms already find it worth their while to subscribe to such computerized services, which do not come cheap. The present systems will, no doubt, seem outmoded and primitive within a few years.

5. On Llewellyn's historical work, see, in addition to *The Common Law Tradition: Deciding Appeals* (1960), his casebook and articles on sales law which are discussed in Chapter 4 *supra*, text at and following note 36. On the historical thesis of *The Common Law Tradition*, see Chapter 1 *supra*, §IV.

6. I have deliberately used the cumbersome phrase "what has

come to be called legal history" in order to give myself the opportunity to express my disapproval of the term "legal history."
The only legal materials that are or ever have been or ever will be
available are historical—cases that have already been decided,
statutes that have already been enacted, and so on. There is ab-
solutely no point in setting up a separate category of legal writing
(or law teaching) to be known as "legal history." To the extent
that we segregate the study of our legal past from the study of our
legal present, we become not historians but antiquarians.

7. The emphasis on procedural regularity and the following
of precedents in the academic version of the Rule of Law idea
suggests that we are dealing with a survival (or revival) of nineteenth-century formalism. I do not know exactly when the Rule
of Law tag, as a shorthand expression for these ideas, came into
use or who first used it. My best memory is that the tag had acquired the exalted status of a cliché by the mid-1950s. The people
who promoted the Rule of Law in the 1950s may be taken as fore-
runners of the New Conceptualists of the 1970s, whose work will
presently be discussed in the text.

8. See, however, the final paragraph of note 11 *infra*.

9. *The Death of Contract* 103 (1974).

10. See Chapter 4 *supra*, §III.

11. See, for example, the work of Professor Richard Posner of
the University of Chicago Law School, two examples of which are
cited Chapter 3 *supra*, note 35. The *Journal of Legal Studies*, which
Professor Posner has edited since it was founded in 1972, has
published a great deal of material of this sort. At the end of the
second issue Professor Posner contributed an Afterword in which
he explained the purpose of the editors: "The aim of the *Journal*
is to encourage the application of scientific methods to the study
of the legal system. As biology is to living organisms, astronomy
to the stars, or economics to the price system, so should legal
studies be to the legal system: an endeavor to make precise, objective, and systematic observations of how the legal system op-
erates in fact and to discover and explain the recurrent patterns
in the observations—the 'laws' of the system." (Posner, "Volume
One of the Journal of Legal Studies—An Afterword," 1 *J. Legal
Studies* 437 (1972). Cf. the remarks of Dean Langdell in 1886,
quoted Chapter 3 *supra*, text at note 2.

As another example of the New Conceptualism, I would cite the extremely interesting work of Professor Ian Macneil. See, e.g., "The Many Futures of Contracts," 47 *S. Calif. L. Rev.* 691 (1974). I understand that the article cited is the first instalment of (or a precursor to) a major work on contract theory.

Some of the reviews of my lectures, *The Death of Contract* (1974), also seem to me to have been animated by the spirit of the New Conceptualism. See, e.g., the review by Gordley, 89 *Harv. L. Rev.* 452 (1975), in the course of which the author comments (at p. 455): "Professor Gilmore's book is as full of unconscious historical forces as Cotton Mather's book is of spirits riding invisibly on wind and water," citing C. Mather, *The Wonders of the Invisible World* (1693). Evidently the game of "Who's a Conceptualist?" is one that two can play. See also Mooney, "The Rise and Fall of Classical Contract Law: A Response to Professor Gilmore," 55 *Ore. L. Rev.* 155 (1976). Professor Mooney does me the great honor of accurately stating my ideas before proceeding, quite properly, to attack them. He collects the citations of other reviews in which the merits of my thesis have been questioned. For my own unrepentant views, see Chapter 3 *supra*, note 8.

My linking of the New Conceptualism with the "conservative reaction which inspired the political slogans [of the 1950s]" may not be altogether accurate. Much of the recent writing which I would lump under that rubric does seem to proceed from the extreme right wing (speaking both politically and jurisprudentially) but by no means all of it. Certainly, a fondness for unitary theory and universal abstraction has never been the exclusive possession of conservative thinkers. See, for an obvious example, the work of the late Karl Marx.

12. See Chapter 3 *supra*, text at note 16.

Index

Activism, judicial. *See* Courts
Admiralty law: federalization of
(pre–Civil War period), 30;
developments in (since World
War II), 92 *n*48, 97 *n*58
American Bar Association: and
the codification of commercial
law after *1900*, 69–70
American law: its beginnings,
8–11; its relationship with
English law, 9–11, 19 *et seq.;*
periods of (since *1800*), 11;
roles of state and federal law
under the federal Constitution,
20–21; influence of the frontier
spirit on, 21–22; hostility to
England, 22; its professionalization after *1820*, 23; influence of
Lord Mansfield on its development, 24; the problem of
national uniformity, 25 *et seq.;*
the pre–Civil War literature, 27
et seq.; the Supreme Court and
federalization (pre–Civil War),
30 *et seq.;* doctrine of *Swift* v.
Tyson (q.v.), 31 *et seq.;*
de Tocqueville on, 35; judicial
power (pre–Civil War period),
35; slavery (its effect on
development of), 36 *et seq.;*
pre–Civil War law and
classical Roman law
analogized, 39; establishment of
the national reporter system
(*1880s*) and its effects, 58–59;

the Langdellian literature,
59–60; the judicial product in
the pre–Civil War period, 60
et seq.; the apparent death of
the federal law principle
(*Erie R.R.* v. *Tompkins*), 93;
rebirth of the federal law
principle in the post-*Erie*
period, 93–95. *See also*
Codification; Courts;
Formalism
American Law Institute: and the
Restatements of the law, 72;
sponsor of Uniform Commercial
Code, 83; its membership, 84
Assumpsit. *See* Contract, law of

Bentham, Jeremy (*1748–1831*):
his advocacy of codification,
25–26
Blackstone, William (*1723–1780*):
his *Commentaries on the Law of
England* discussed, 5; his
Commentaries compared with
the American Restatements, 73
Brandeis, Louis Dembitz
(*1856–1941*): his career, 69 *n*3

Cardozo, Benjamin Nathan
(*1870–1938*): as a symbol, 74;
his judicial technique, 75; his
lectures on *The Nature of the
Judicial Process*, 75–77
Codification: Bentham on, 25–26;
the pre–Civil War codification

Law: as a social science, 3, 87–88;
and social change, 14, 110;
as a science (Dean Langdell's
formulation), 42–43; as a
science (Holmes on), 50; the
18th-century social science
hypothesis questioned, 99–101;
as a science (Professòr Posner's
formulation), 108 *n*11;
limitations of, 109–11. *See also*
Formalism; Legal Realism
Law schools: their first appearance
in this country, 19; the
introduction of case method
teaching by Dean Langdell,
43 *n*3; reorganization of
Harvard Law School by Dean
Langdell, 57; their influence
(late 19th century), 57–58; the
triumph of Legal Realism in,
86–87; their recruitment of
social scientists, 87–88; and
empirical studies in law, 89;
growth of interest in legal
history since *1960*, 103–04
Legal history: growth of interest
in since *1960*, 102–04
Legal Realism: the Realist
controversy discussed, 77–80;
its triumph in the law schools,
86–87; acceptance of basic
tenets of Langdellian
formalism, 87; and the social
sciences, 87–88; attitudes
toward codification, 90–91;
attitudes toward the New Deal,
90–91; hostility toward the
judicial process, 90–91, 92
Llewellyn, Karl Nickerson
(*1893–1962*): his "periodization"
of American legal history, 11;
The Common Law Tradition, 11;
on the Grand Style in pre–Civil

War American cases, 39; his
part in the Legal Realist
controversy, 78; his work as an
example of pluralism, 81–83;
his role as Chief Reporter for
Uniform Commercial Code,
83–86; his theory of
codification, 85

McDougal, Myres S.: his policy
science system of jurisprudence,
89–90
Mansfield, First Earl of (William
Murray) (*1705–1793*): his
contribution to the development
of English law, 7; rejection of
his theories in England after his
death, 8; his influence on
American law, 24
Maritime law. *See* Admiralty law
Murray, William (First Earl of
Mansfield). *See* Mansfield

National Conference of
Commissioners on Uniform
State Laws: and the codification
of commercial law after *1900*,
69; sponsor of Uniform
Commercial Code, 83; its
membership, 84
National Reporter System: its
establishment (*1880s*) and the
effect thereof, 58–59
Negotiable Instruments Law: its
emergence following the
industrial revolution, 6;
codification of, 69

Peirce, Charles (*1839–1914*): his
ideas on scientific inquiry, 50;
his relationship with Holmes, 50
Pluralism: as characteristic of the

154

INDEX

Tocqueville, Alexis de (*1805–1859*): on the American approach to law, 35

Tort: 19th-century development of theory, 46; the post–World War II products liability cases, 92 *n*48

Uniform Commercial Code: role of Llewellyn as Chief Reporter, 83–84; discussed, 83–86; jurisprudence of, 85–86; as a compromise which satisfied no one, 85–86; its enactment, 86; *1972* revision of Article 9, 96 *n*56

Uniform Revised Sales Act: incorporated in Uniform Commercial Code, 83

Uniform Sales Act: and the post-*1900* codification movement, 69; drafted by Samuel Williston, 71; and Williston's treatise on sales, 71; its style of drafting, 71–72; attacked by Llewellyn, 82–83

Williston, Samuel (*1861–1963*): draftsman of Uniform Sales Act, 71; his treatise on sales, 71 *n*12; his treatise on contracts, 71 *n*12, 80 *n*29; Chief Reporter of *Restatement of Contracts*, 73; his work in sales law attacked by Llewellyn, 82

World Peace through World Law: the slogan discussed, 105–06